A Midsummer Night's Dream

SERIES EDITOR:
JOHN SEELY

EDITORIAL MATERIAL AND ACTIVITIES:
ELIZABETH SEELY
RICHARD DURANT
JOHN SEELY

Part of Pearson

Heinemann is an imprint of Pearson Education Limited, a company incorporated in England and Wales, having its registered office at Edinburgh Gate, Harlow, Essex, CM20 2JE. Registered company number: 872828

www.pearsonschoolsandfecolleges.co.uk

Heinemann is a registered trademark of Pearson Education Limited

Editorial material and activities © John Seely Partnership and Richard Durant 2010
All other material © Pearson Education Limited 2010

The right of John Seely Partnership and Richard Durant to be identified as the authors of this work has been asserted by them in accordance with the Copyright, Designs and Patents Act 1988.

First published 1994
This new edition published 2010

12 11 10
10 9 8 7 6 5 4 3 2 1

British Library Cataloguing in Publication Data
A catalogue record for this book is available from the British Library
.
ISBN 9780435026462

Typeset by Redmoor Design, Tavistock, Devon
Original illustrations © Pearson Education Limited, 2005
Illustrated by Roger Wade Walker
Cover photo © Photostage Ltd
Printed and bound in China (CTPS/01)

Every effort has been made to contact copyright holders of material reproduced in this book. Any omissions will be rectified in subsequent printings if notice is given to the publishers.

CONTENTS

The story of the play

Act 1

Scene 1

Theseus, Duke of Athens, and Hippolyta are looking forward to their wedding in four days' time.

Their happy mood is interrupted by the arrival of Egeus and his daughter Hermia, and two young men, Lysander and Demetrius, both of whom want to marry her. Egeus complains to the Duke that his daughter is refusing to marry Demetrius, her father's choice. Egeus demands the death penalty for her disobedience.

Hermia is in love with Lysander. She insists, even to the Duke, that she will not marry Demetrius. Lysander points out that Demetrius had previously been in love with another young woman called Helena, but he has changed his mind.

Theseus tells Hermia that she must either obey her father and marry Demetrius or be put to death. He cannot make her change her decision, but tells her the penalty is either death or life in a convent. He warns her that she will not be happy as a nun, and gives her the four days until his own wedding to make her choice.

Hermia and Lysander agree that they will meet in the wood the following evening and will go to Lysander's aunt's house, where, away from the power of Athenian law, they can safely be married. They tell Helena, who is Hermia's childhood friend, of their plan. She is still desperately in love with Demetrius and decides to betray them to him and then go to the wood herself, so that she can at least be near him.

Scene 2

Six Athenian workmen have been chosen to put on a play for the royal wedding celebrations. They hold a meeting to cast their play, which is a tragedy about the forbidden love and the death of the lovers Pyramus and Thisby. Although Peter Quince, a carpenter, is in charge and has cast the play, Bottom, a weaver, keeps interrupting and is full of ideas about every part that is mentioned. They arrange to meet in the wood for their rehearsal, so that their plans will remain a secret.

Act 2

Scene 1

Puck, who is the servant of Oberon, the Fairy King, meets a fairy who serves Titania, the Fairy Queen. Puck explains that the fairy kingdom has been split by a serious quarrel between Oberon and Titania over the ownership of a stolen Indian child. Oberon wants the boy to be one of his pages and Titania refuses to give him up. The fairy recognises Puck as the sprite who is famous for playing practical jokes on humans. He can make himself invisible or take on different shapes.

Oberon and Titania meet, still quarrelling. Titania claims that as a result of their dispute, the weather and the seasons are all at odds and humans are suffering. She explains why she wants to keep the child.

Oberon decides to punish Titania and force her to part with the boy. He uses Puck to fetch a magic flower. When the juice of this plant is squeezed on sleeping eyelids, the man or woman treated with it will fall madly in love with the first creature seen on awaking.

Oberon watches Helena and Demetrius together. She is still chasing Demetrius and will not leave him alone although he speaks very cruelly to her. Oberon tells Puck to treat Demetrius with the juice so that he will fall in love with Helena.

Scene 2

Titania's fairies lull her to sleep and set a guard, but Oberon steals in and squeezes the magic juice on Titania's eyelids.

Hermia and Lysander have lost their way in the wood and decide to sleep until morning. Because they are not yet married, Hermia will not let Lysander sleep very close to her. While they are asleep Puck mistakenly applies the juice to Lysander's eyes, thinking he is Demetrius.

Helena can no longer keep up with Demetrius. Left behind, she sees Lysander lying on the ground and, thinking he may be wounded or dead, wakes him up. The result of Puck's mistake is that Lysander now falls madly in love with Helena, who thinks it is all a pretence and done to make fun of her. Lysander leaves Hermia asleep on the ground, saying he hates her now, and follows Helena. Hermia then wakes up from a nightmare in which a snake was eating her heart, while Lysander looked on, smiling. She is very anxious and hurt that Lysander has left her without a word.

Act 3
Scene 1

Without realising it, the Athenian workmen are rehearsing near where Titania is sleeping. Puck chances on the workmen's rehearsal. This gives him an idea to help Oberon in his plans and he puts an ass's head on Bottom who is waiting for his cue. When Bottom's friends see it they run off in terror and Puck leads them around the wood, taking on different shapes. Bottom sings to show he is not afraid. This wakes Titania up and she falls in love with him. She gives him fairies to wait on him, and they go away together.

Scene 2

Puck tells Oberon what has happened to Titania and he is very pleased. He is not so pleased, however, when he realises that Puck has put the juice on the wrong Athenian lover's eyes.

Hermia, abandoned by Lysander, has gone off in search of him but finds Demetrius, who is still in love with her. He is looking for Lysander so that he can kill him.

Hermia accuses Demetrius of having already killed Lysander. He denies it. They quarrel and, when she runs off, Demetrius falls asleep. Oberon sends Puck to bring Helena along and puts the juice on Demetrius' eyes at last.

Lysander is desperately trying to prove to Helena how much he loves her. He is in tears. She insists that Hermia is the one he loves and is sure it is all a cruel joke. Helena and Lysander argue so loudly that they wake Demetrius. The first person he sees is Helena and he declares his love for her.

When Hermia comes looking for Lysander, she too is bewildered, but Helena thinks they are all in a plot to make a fool of her. Soon there is a four-sided quarrel going on. It becomes so serious that Hermia tries to claw Helena's face with her nails, and Lysander and Demetrius go off to fight a duel over Helena. The two women, angry and hurt, go off in different directions.

Oberon will not allow a duel to result from Puck's mistake and sends him to lead the two men astray. He keeps them apart till they lie down to sleep from exhaustion. Soon Hermia and Helena separately find the same spot in the dark and they too fall asleep. Puck treats Lysander's eyes with the juice of another plant. This is the antidote to the love-juice.

Act 4
Scene 1

Oberon watches the results of his revenge on Titania while she sleeps with Bottom asleep in her arms. He criticised her earlier about her infatuation with Bottom. Now she has given up the child to him. He removes the magic with the antidote and they are happy together again. Puck is instructed to remove the ass's head from Bottom, and to lay a deep sleep over him and the four lovers.

Theseus and Hippolyta, with some of their courtiers, including Egeus, are out early in the forest to celebrate Midsummer Day and to go hunting. Theseus proudly shows off his hounds to his fiancée, who knows a lot about the subject. They stumble on the four lovers, and wake them up.

Egeus is furious when he learns that Lysander and Hermia had planned to elope, but Demetrius declares his love for Helena. So Theseus, realising that the couples are now happily paired, decides that this is the right outcome. He announces that all three couples shall be married at a triple wedding ceremony. Still bewildered, they all follow the Duke. Bottom, with ass's head removed, wakes up, still under the influence of his amazing experience. He feels it was a 'most rare vision' and wants Quince to write a ballad about it.

Scene 2

The other workmen are very concerned at Bottom's disappearance, because without him their play cannot be put on. They also think the Duke might have rewarded them for their performance. Bottom arrives back just in time for the play to go ahead. He promises to tell them his story later and tells them to get ready for the play.

Act 5
Scene 1

Theseus and Hippolyta are discussing the lovers' story. Theseus puts it down to tricks of the imagination but Hippolyta is more inclined to think that something odd really did happen.

Theseus greets the lovers and considers which of the many possible entertainments to have that evening. Philostrate has seen the workmen's play in rehearsal and advises against it, but Theseus overrules him since it has been prepared with love and a sense of duty.

The workmen present their play with the court and the lovers commenting on it – Bottom in the role of Pyramus returns from the dead to comment on their comments. They follow their play with a dance. It is after midnight and Theseus suggests it is time for bed. There will be two weeks of celebrations.

Puck prepares the way for Oberon and Titania. The Fairy King and Queen and all their followers dance through the house bringing blessings to all the newly-weds, and any children they may have.

Puck brings the play to an end, apologising for any offence given and claiming that all the action can be regarded as a dream.

Separate strands of the story

It is quite easy to get confused by the story of *A Midsummer Night's Dream*. This is partly because it is not really one story, but four. On the following pages, these four stories are told separately.

Theseus and Hippolyta

Act 1 scene 1

Theseus, Duke of Athens, and Hippolyta, Queen of the Amazons, are looking forward to their wedding in four days' time. Great celebrations are planned.

Egeus brings a complaint against his daughter, Hermia. He has chosen Demetrius as a husband for her but she is in love with someone else – Lysander. Egeus is demanding her obedience or her death.

Theseus tells Hermia she should obey her father. By law she must choose between obedience, death, or life as a nun. She must give her choice on Theseus' wedding day.

When Theseus is reminded that Demetrius has previously been in love with a girl called Helena, who still worships him, he takes Demetrius and Egeus off for private conversation.

Act 4 scene 1

Early on Midsummer morning Theseus and Hippolyta are out in the woods. They intend to hunt, but suddenly they stumble across the four lovers, fast asleep. Egeus is furious that Lysander and Hermia had meant to run away, but Theseus, realising that all four are now happily paired, overrules Egeus and suggests a joint wedding ceremony.

Act 5 scene 1

Hippolyta and Theseus, now married, discuss the lovers' stories about the previous night. He thinks it is all imagination; she believes them.

Intrigued by the contradictions it offers, Theseus chooses the workmen's play 'Pyramus and Thisby' for the evening's entertainment. He assures Hippolyta that he has learned to understand people's intentions, rather than their success or failure. They both comment on the play, wittily but not cruelly. It is after midnight when Theseus thanks the players and brings the evening to a close, promising a fortnight of celebrations.

Lysander and Hermia, Demetrius and Helena

Act 1 scene 1

Hermia is brought to the court by her father, Egeus, because she refuses to marry her father's choice for her, Demetrius. She is deeply in love with Lysander, whom Egeus will not accept. Egeus insists on her obedience or her death. Theseus confirms that the law demands her obedience, her death, or life as a nun. Lysander and Demetrius state their claim. Lysander says Demetrius has previously been in love with Helena, who still worships him. Hermia is left to make her decision within the next four days. Lysander and Hermia agree to run away together to his aunt's house, and marry where Athenian law cannot reach them. They will meet the following night in the wood. Helena is very unhappy that Demetrius no longer loves her and is both jealous and envious of Hermia. Lysander and Hermia tell Helena of their plans, but she then decides to betray them to Demetrius and follow him into the wood.

Act 2 scene 1

Helena chases Demetrius through the wood. He speaks cruelly to her and goes off to find and kill Lysander, still followed by Helena. Oberon, the Fairy King, has been watching this, takes pity on Helena and tells Puck to treat Demetrius' eyes with magic love-juice.

Act 2 scene 2

Lysander and Hermia lose their way in the wood and decide to sleep until daylight. Hermia will not let Lysander lie too close.

Puck, who is actually looking for Demetrius, finds Lysander and doses his eyes with magic juice by mistake. The juice will make Lysander fall desperately in love with the first creature he sees when he wakes up.

Helena can no longer keep up with Demetrius. She sees Lysander lying on the ground and wakes him up. He instantly falls in love with her. She believes he is mocking her and goes. Before Lysander follows her, he stands over the still-sleeping Hermia saying how much he hates her. Hermia wakes up from a nightmare. She is alarmed that Lysander has disappeared and goes off to find him.

Act 3 scene 2

Hermia comes in with Demetrius. She is looking for Lysander and assumes that Demetrius has killed him. She invites him to kill her too. Demetrius says he is innocent. She leaves.

Demetrius is tired out and lies down to sleep. Oberon takes this opportunity to put the magic juice on his eyes. Meanwhile Lysander, in tears, is trying to convince Helena of his love. She will not believe it because she knows he loves Hermia. While they are arguing Demetrius wakes up and falls in love with Helena. She thinks they've teamed up to make fun of her. Hermia now joins them, delighted at finding Lysander. She is shocked and hurt when he says he hates her now. Helena thinks she is part of the conspiracy to mock her.

Now both Lysander and Demetrius are rivals for Helena's love. They decide to fight a duel. The women turn on each other and nearly fight but Helena runs away and Hermia leaves.

Puck leads the men apart in a magic fog. First Lysander lies down, exhausted, and falls asleep, then Demetrius. Helena, worn out, lies down too, and finally Hermia. All are in the same clearing, but all unseen by the others. Puck applies the antidote to the love-juice to Lysander's eyes.

Act 4 scene 1

When the huntsmen wake them, Lysander tries to explain matters to the Duke. Egeus wants Lysander punished, but Demetrius now declares that Helena is his only true love for ever. The Duke tells Egeus the lovers should stay happily paired, as they are. They follow the Duke back to Athens and are married.

Titania, Oberon, and Puck

Act 2 scene 1

Puck, Oberon's servant, meets one of Titania's fairies. Puck is famous for playing tricks on humans, but can bring good luck too.

Titania and Oberon have quarrelled over the possession of an Indian child. Oberon wants Titania to give him the boy as one of his attendants. She has refused. Oberon and Titania meet. They have come because of the royal wedding and they accuse one another of having loved Hippolyta and Theseus. Titania claims that all the seasons have been at odds since their squabble. She refuses to part with the boy and explains why. They part, still very angry.

Oberon plans to blackmail her into parting with the child. He tells Puck to fetch a magic flower, the juice of which, laid on sleeping eyes, will make the victim fall hopelessly in love with the first creature seen. There is an antidote which can remove the charm.

While Puck is away, Oberon watches Demetrius being unkind to Helena and decides that Puck shall put some of the magic juice on Demetrius' eyes.

Once Oberon has the juice he finds Titania asleep and applies the juice to her eyes.

Puck mistakes Lysander for Demetrius and so puts the juice on Lysander's eyes.

Act 3 scene 1

Puck watches the workmen's play rehearsal and puts an ass's head on Bottom. Titania falls in love with Bottom. Oberon is delighted when Puck tells him what he has done. When Oberon and Puck watch Hermia and Demetrius they realise that Puck has treated the wrong man. Oberon is angry with Puck and sends him to fetch Helena. Meanwhile Oberon treats the eyelids of the sleeping Demetrius. He and Puck watch as both Demetrius and Lysander declare their love for Helena and she rejects it all as cruel mockery. When Demetrius and Lysander go off, intending to fight a duel, Puck is told to create a magic fog and to keep them apart. When all the lovers have lain down to sleep he squeezes the juice on Lysander's eyes.

Act 4 scene 1

Oberon watches Titania with Bottom. He feels both jealousy and pity.
As she has given him the child he will release her from the spell. Puck
is to release Bottom also. Oberon wakes Titania, who now loathes
the sight of Bottom. A deep sleep is laid over the lovers and Bottom.
Friends again, Oberon and Titania dance.

Act 5 scene 1

Puck comes to prepare the house for the fairies. Oberon, Titania and
the fairies bless the house, the marriages and the future children of all
three couples. Puck ends the play with an apology for any offence and
the suggestion that perhaps the audience has been dreaming too.

Bottom and the workmen

Act 1 scene 2

Six Athenian workmen meet to discuss putting on a play as part of the royal wedding celebrations. The play is about the forbidden love of Pyramus and Thisby. Quince is the producer and he gives the part of Pyramus to Bottom, the weaver. Having cast the play they agree to meet on the following evening in the wood.

Act 3 scene 1

They meet near where Titania is asleep. To avoid frightening their audience they must explain away the sword and the lion. They start rehearsing, misreading words and ignoring their cues.

Puck comes past and stays to watch. After Bottom's first exit Puck puts an ass's head on him. All Bottom's friends run away in terror and Puck plans to lead them all around the dark wood. Bottom stays and sings to keep his courage up. Titania hears him and falls in love with him. She gives him fairies to wait on him and takes him away with her.

Act 4 scene 1

Titania is caressing her new love. She offers him music and food. He prefers things he is used to. Soon he falls asleep in her arms. While Bottom sleeps, Oberon takes the charm off Titania's eyes and Puck removes the ass's head from Bottom. He is still in a magically deep sleep. When he wakes up he remembers the strange things he has seen and feels the need to write about it.

Bottom's friends are very concerned about him. Bottom suddenly reappears, promising to tell them his story, but hustling them to get ready for the play.

Act 5 scene 1

The workmen's play is to be the evening's entertainment. In the prologue Quince says the opposite of what the speech means, because he is so nervous. All the characters are introduced and the play goes ahead. The audience is entertained and comments freely. A couple of times Bottom cannot help putting the Duke right. Bottom clearly enjoys the role of Pyramus and his bloody death. Theseus chooses a dance to end the programme. The players are thanked and leave.

Background to the play

A Midsummer Night's Dream was first performed in 1595 or 1596. At this time, the Chamberlain's Men, the theatrical company to which Shakespeare belonged, performed at The Theatre. They did not move to the Globe until 1599. The play first appeared in print in 1600.

Shakespeare and comedy

Nowadays we expect the plays we see on TV to follow a particular pattern: sitcom, hospital drama, soap, and so on. Similarly in Shakespeare's time the audience expected plays to belong to a particular genre. If, like *A Midsummer Night's Dream*, the play was described as a comedy then it was required to follow certain patterns.

The commonest pattern concerned the struggle between young and old. Two young lovers wanted to marry but were prevented by an old man, usually the young woman's father. The main part of the play would follow the lovers' struggles as they attempted to overcome this obstacle, usually finding themselves more and more entangled by the things that happened to them. Then, in the final act, all their problems would be overcome and they would live happily ever after.

Many of Shakespeare's comedies take this pattern and *A Midsummer Night's Dream* is no exception. We have the obstinate old father, Egeus, who tells his daughter Hermia that she may not marry the man she is in love with, Lysander. Instead, she has to marry the man he has chosen, Demetrius. But Shakespeare makes the story more complicated by introducing another young woman, Helena, who just happens to be in love with Demetrius.

Love and marriage

Hermia, Helena, Lysander, and Demetrius are not, however, the only characters who have problems with their relationships. Act 2 begins with a major disagreement between Oberon and Titania. She has found a 'changeling' boy on whom she dotes, and Oberon wants this boy for himself. She refuses and goes off on her own. Oberon decides to punish her and get the boy by using magic. In the end he succeeds, so confirming that men get their own way in the end.

This attitude towards the sexes seems to be shared by Theseus. In classical mythology Theseus had the reputation of being a serial womaniser, using brute force when he couldn't achieve what he wanted any other way. In this play, Theseus hasn't courted Hippolyta in the ordinary way – he has won her in battle. She is his captive.

We have to remember, too, that Hippolyta was the Queen of the Amazons. They were warrior women who lived in a society where men had little place and no power. Such a society would have been alien and threatening to macho 'heroes' like Theseus (and to domineering fathers like Egeus). So it's revealing that in the end Theseus overrules Egeus and allows Hermia to marry Lysander, even though her father has the law on his side.

The idea of a male-dominated society would have been taken for granted by most people in Shakespeare's time. So would the assumption that a father had the right to decide whom his daughter should marry. This is not to say that fathers always forced their daughters to marry men they didn't love. In fact, much of the time young women were able to marry for love – but only after their parents had checked that the young man they wanted to marry was of the right social class and economic status. And, of course, there were plenty of occasions when young couples had to marry because a baby was on the way, which is exactly what happened to Shakespeare as a young man.

Midsummer's Eve

The conflict between the young lovers and Egeus is the motor that drives the comedy along. However, Shakespeare introduces many other elements to complicate the plot. His sixteenth century audience would have been warned of some of these by the play's title.

Since pre-Christian times, the midsummer solstice has had a special importance to people all over the world. In the English countryside it was celebrated on June 24th, St John's Eve, as a festival of fertility. Huge bonfires were lit and the shortest night of the year was celebrated with music and dancing. The revellers would jump through the flames to ensure good luck, and they would be entertained by morris dancers and performances of traditional plays. Above all, it was a time when the usual rules of polite society did not apply.

Dreams

Just as today, in Shakespeare's time people were fascinated by dreams: where do they come from? What do they mean? Do they foretell the future? Generally people considered that some dreams could indeed foretell the future and many books were published offering to explain what particular dreams prophesied. Other dreams, they thought, were just the result of things that have happened to us: if you have spent all day watching and thinking about horror films, then it isn't surprising if you have nightmares.

But Shakespeare seems to be saying that the whole of the play is a kind of dream. At the end Puck says, that 'this weak and idle theme' is 'no more yielding than a dream'. In other words it means as little – or as much – as a dream. When the lovers have woken up at the end of Act 4 scene 1 and all their troubles have been overcome, Demetrius asks:

> *Are you sure*
> *That we are awake? It seems to me*
> *That yet we sleep, we dream.*

However, some very real things have happened to them. To say the least, they have been rather unkind to each other at different stages. Perhaps, too, they have learned some unexpected things about themselves, and that, too, is something that can happen in dreams.

So by calling this play a 'dream', Shakespeare leads us to ask ourselves just what is going on as we watch or read the play.

Fairies and magic

Another feature of St John's Eve was that it was a night when you were especially likely to encounter fairies. In the Middle Ages, belief in fairies was common. They were a convenient way of explaining things that otherwise couldn't be explained: from milk going off to children being born deformed. On the whole, most of the things that were put down to fairies tended to be unpleasant or even evil. Above all, they were believed to pinch you.

On the other hand, Peaseblossom, Cobweb and the others are kind to Bottom when he meets them. They seem to be 'good' fairies. But Puck is different. He certainly does some of things that were typically blamed on fairies, for example playing tricks on an old woman, making her spill her drink and fall down on 'her bum'. Yet he is more powerful. He can become invisible, and travel very fast:

> *I'll put a girdle round about the earth*
> *In forty minutes.*

Puck can only do what his master, Oberon, commands him. Between them, they work magic on the young lovers, with varying degrees of success. Once again, this is good magic, or is meant to be. Even Titania comes out of her bewitchment none the worse for her experience of falling in love with a creature who is half man, half donkey.

Shakespeare's theatre

Nowadays entertainment is piped into people's houses – TV, the internet and radio provide hundreds of different programme choices every day. But in Shakespeare's time, people went out to be entertained. If you lived in a city like London you could go to the theatre.

But it wasn't the kind of theatre we know today. There was no electricity and the only artificial lighting was candles or torches, so plays had to be watched in daylight. This meant that the main part of the theatre was open to the skies.

Many of Shakespeare's plays were performed at the Globe Theatre. A modern replica of the Globe now stands on London's Bankside, close to where the original was built. By visiting the Globe Theatre you can discover what it was like to go to the theatre in Shakespeare's time.

Once you were inside, you would see that the ground plan was more or less circular: in *Henry V*, Shakespeare talks about 'the wooden O'. All around the outside were galleries where people could pay to sit on a wooden bench. From the galleries you looked down on the stage and – very important – you were under cover if it rained!

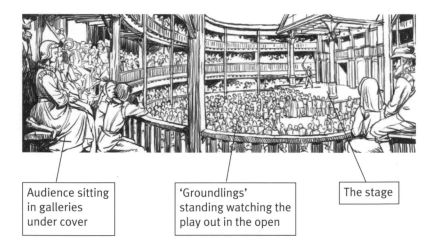

| Audience sitting in galleries under cover | 'Groundlings' standing watching the play out in the open | The stage |

The stage measured about 12 metres by 12 metres. It was raised about 1.5 metres above the ground and was surrounded by a wide standing area. This was where the 'groundlings' went to watch the play. It was the cheapest way of seeing a play, but it meant that you had to stand for anything up to three hours. On the other hand, you were much closer to the action – the people at the front were close enough to touch the actors when they came to the edge of the stage.

As you will see when you read the play, Shakespeare often gives the characters **soliloquies**, speeches which they make when alone on stage. Often they seem to be deliberately sharing their thoughts with the audience. When you look at the stage of the Globe and see how close the audience was, you realise how effective this must have been.

Some modern theatres have a curtain which hides the stage from the audience before the play and between scenes. This makes it easy to change the scenery without the audience seeing what is going on. In Shakespeare's theatre there was no curtain to conceal the main stage; the stage was always open to the audience. Very little scenery was used and if furniture was needed, the actors had to carry it on themselves. Similarly, if a character died on stage, the body had to be carried off as part of the action.

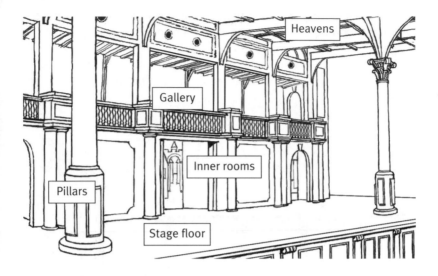

The stage was, however, quite complicated. Two large pillars on the main lower stage supported the roof, which was known as the 'heavens'. This kept the actors dry if it rained, but it could also be used for the action of the play. In some of the plays, Shakespeare has characters lowered from above down onto the stage. There were also trapdoors in the stage itself, so that people could suddenly appear from below. The heavens contained a space which could be used for sound effects. Cannons could be fired for battle scenes and cannon balls rolled along the floor to make the sound of thunder. At the back of the stage there was an inner room which could be concealed by a curtain. This was sometimes used for short scenes in the play.

Shakespeare's language

It is easy to look at the text of this play and say to yourself, 'I'm never going to understand that!' but it is important not to be put off. Remember that there are two reasons why Shakespeare's language may seem strange at first:

1 He was writing 400 years ago and the English language has changed over the centuries.

2 He wrote mainly in **verse**. As a result he sometimes changed the order of words to make them fit the verse form, and he used a large number of 'tricks of the trade': figures of speech and other techniques.

Language change

This can cause three main kinds of problem:

Grammar

Since the end of the sixteenth century, there have been some changes in English grammar. Some examples:

1 *Thee, thou, thy,* and the verb forms that go with them:
   *What **thou seest** when **thou dost** wake,*
   *Do it for **thy** true-love take;*
   Love and languish for his sake.
   *...When **thou wakest**, it is **thy** dear.*
   Wake when some vile thing is near.
   (Act 2 scene 2 lines 27–34)

2 Words contract (shorten) in different ways. For example:
   'tis rather than *it's*
   who is't for *who is it*
   So we get a line like this:
   'Tis strange my Theseus, that these lovers speak of.
   (Act 5 scene 1 lines 1–2)

3 Some of the 'little words' are different, such as *an* for *if*.
   For example Bottom says:
   ***An** I may hide my face, let me play Thisby too.*
   He means that **if** he can wear a veil or mask, he can also play the part of Thisby.

Words that have changed their meaning

Sometimes you will come across words that you think you know, but then discover that they don't mean what you expect them to mean. For example: 'saucy' (Act 5 scene 1 line 103) meant insulting, insolent in Shakespeare's day. Now it means cheeky. Nowadays 'presently' means shortly, in a moment or two. But in Act 4 scene 2 line 36, it means immediately, without a moment's delay.

Words that have gone out of use

These are the most obvious and most frequent causes of difficulty. Shakespeare had – and used – a huge vocabulary. He loved using words, and pushing them to their limits. So you will come across many words you have not met before. These are explained in the notes on the page facing the play text.

Verse and prose

A Midsummer Night's Dream is written in a mixture of **rhymed verse**, **blank verse**, and **prose**.

Rhymed verse

Over half of *A Midsummer Night's Dream* is written in verse lines that rhyme. The play's rhyming verse takes several forms and is used in a variety of ways. The lovers often speak to each other in rhymed lines. These have ten syllables and a regular pattern of weak and strong syllables:

*In **that** same **place** thou **hast** ap**point**ed **me**,*
*To**mor**row **tru**ly **will** I **meet** with **thee**.*

The line divides into five sections, each with a weak and a strong beat. This is called an **iambic pentameter**.

Rhyme can make some speeches very stylised and almost ritualistic. For example when Hermia promises Lysander that she will elope with him in Act 1 scene 1:

HERMIA   By the simplicity of Venus' doves,
              By that which knitteth souls, and prospers loves,
              And by that fire which burned the Carthage queen,
              When the false Troyan under sail was seen,
              By all the vows that ever men have broke,
              In number more than even women spoke,

> In that same place thou hast appointed me,
> Tomorrow truly will I meet with thee.

(lines 171–8)

In this speech pairs of lines are rhymed. (These are called 'rhyming couplets'.) At other points in the play speeches are written so that every other line rhymes:

LYSANDER   Why should you think that I should woo in scorn?
             Scorn and derision never come in tears.
             Look when I vow, I weep; and vows so born,
             In their nativity all truth appears.

(Act 3 scene 2 lines 122–5)

Rhyme is used in the magic world of Oberon and Titania:

OBERON   What thou seest when thou dost wake,
             Do it for thy true-love take;
             Love and languish for his sake.
             Be it ounce, or cat, or bear,
             Pard, or boar with bristled hair,
             In thy eye that shall appear
             When thou wakest, it is thy dear.
             Wake when some vile thing is near.

(Act 2 scene 2 lines 27–34)

Here the lines are shorter. If you count the syllables you will find that each line has seven syllables. (In fact these are 14-syllable lines, or 'fourteeners', split into two shorter lines.) This is the commonest pattern for the rhymed lines in the world of the fairies.

Blank verse

Part of the play is written in iambic pentameters that do not rhyme. This type of verse is called **blank verse**.

Metre and rhythm

If Shakespeare had made every line exactly the same, the play would soon become very monotonous, so he varies the **rhythm** in a number of ways. Often he just changes the pattern of weak and strong slightly:

*Tarry, rash **wan**ton. **Am** I **not** thy **lord**?*
(**tum** ti ti **tum** ti **tum** ti **tum** ti **tum**)

In some parts of the play the variations are much more frequent and obvious. For example, try reading this speech aloud to see the effect it can have:

HERMIA   Puppet? Why so? Ay, that way goes the game.
Now I perceive that she hath made compare
Between our statures, she hath urged her height,
And with her personage, her tall personage,
Her height, forsooth, she hath prevailed with him.
And are you grown so high in his esteem,
Because I am so dwarfish and so low?
How low am I, thou painted maypole? Speak;
How low am I? I am not yet so low,
But that my nails can reach unto thine eyes.

(Act 3 scene 2 lines 289–98)

The pattern of strong and weak beats is varied to help the actress playing Hermia express her anger at the way she thinks she is being treated by Helena.

Prose

There are several quite long sections of *A Midsummer Night's Dream* that are not written in blank or rhymed verse, but are in 'ordinary sentences': **prose**. If you look through the play, you will soon work out that these are the scenes in which Bottom and the workmen appear. In this play, Shakespeare follows the rule that 'noble' characters (and fairies) speak in verse, while the lower classes speak in prose. You will see this when Titania and Bottom are together. She speaks verse, but he speaks prose:

TITANIA   I have a venturous fairy that shall seek
The squirrel's hoard, and fetch thee new nuts.

BOTTOM   I had rather have a handful or two of dried peas.
But, I pray you, let none of your people stir me. I
have an exposition of sleep come upon me.

(Act 4 scene 1 lines 35–9)

A Midsummer Night's Dream

Characters

THESEUS, Duke of Athens

EGEUS, father to Hermia

LYSANDER,
DEMETRIUS, } in love with Hermia

PHILOSTRATE, Master of the Revels to Theseus

PETER QUINCE, a carpenter

SNUG, a joiner

NICK BOTTOM, a weaver

FRANCIS FLUTE, a bellows-mender

TOM SNOUT, a tinker

ROBIN STARVELING, a tailor

HIPPOLYTA, Queen of the Amazons, betrothed to Theseus

HERMIA, daughter to Egeus, in love with Lysander

HELENA, in love with Demetrius

OBERON, King of the fairies

TITANIA, Queen of the fairies

PUCK, or Robin Goodfellow

PEASEBLOSSOM
COBWEB
MOTH } fairies
MUSTARDSEED

Other fairies attending their King and Queen. Attendants on Theseus and Hippolyta

Scene: *Athens, and a wood nearby*

Theseus, Duke of Athens, and Hippolyta are to be married in four days' time and are looking forward to the wedding. They want the whole of Athens to celebrate. Egeus, Hermia's father, arrives.

1–2	**our nuptial … apace** our wedding day will soon be here
2–3	**Four … moon** In four days' time a new month begins
3	**methinks** it seems to me
4	**lingers** delays
5	**step-dame** stepmother
	dowager widow
6	**withering out** wasting away
	revenue income; Theseus has to wait for his wedding-day just as a young man who inherits his father's money may have to wait to enjoy it all himself, because his mother or stepmother still has to use some of it.
7	**steep themselves** be absorbed, lose themselves
10	**behold** see
11	**solemnities** celebrations
13	**pert and nimble** lively and quick, agile
14	**forth** out
15	**The pale … pomp** sadness is not suitable for our ceremony
16–17	**Hippolyta … injuries** Theseus beat the Amazons in battle. Hippolyta was their queen.
18	**in another key** in a completely different tone
19	**pomp** pageantry
	triumph celebration(s)
	revelling entertainment
20	**renowned** famous

Act One

Scene ❶

Athens

Enter THESEUS, HIPPOLYTA, PHILOSTRATE, *and Attendants*

THESEUS
Now, fair Hippolyta, our nuptial hour
Draws on apace. Four happy days bring in
Another moon. But, O, methinks, how slow
This old moon wanes, she lingers my desires,
Like to a step-dame or a dowager, 5
Long withering out a young man's revenue.

HIPPOLYTA
Four days will quickly steep themselves in night,
Four nights will quickly dream away the time;
And then the moon, like to a silver bow
New-bent in heaven, shall behold the night 10
Of our solemnities.

THESEUS
            Go Philostrate,
Stir up the Athenian youth to merriments,
Awake the pert and nimble spirit of mirth,
Turn melancholy forth to funerals;
The pale companion is not for our pomp. 15

[Exit PHILOSTRATE

Hippolyta, I wooed thee with my sword,
And won thy love, doing thee injuries.
But I will wed thee in another key,
With pomp, with triumph, and with revelling.

Enter EGEUS, HERMIA, LYSANDER, *and* DEMETRIUS

EGEUS
Happy be Theseus, our renowned Duke. 20

THESEUS
Thanks, good Egeus. What's the news with thee?

Egeus complains to Theseus that Hermia is refusing to marry Demetrius, who is her father's choice for her. Instead of obeying him she insists she is in love with Lysander and wants to marry him. Athenian law states she must either give in to her father's wishes or face the death penalty. The alternative is to spend the rest of her life in a convent.

22   **vexation** annoyance

27   **bewitched ... child** charmed my daughter's heart

29   **love-tokens** little presents given as a sign of love

30–1 **sung ... love** in a voice pretending to be sincere, sung verses about a love that was not (sincere)

32   **stolen ... fantasy** captured her imagination in a sly way

33   **gauds, conceits** toys and trinkets

34   **Knacks** knick-knacks

      trifles toys or trinkets

      nosegays posies or bunches of flowers

      sweetmeats sweet food, such as sugared cakes, candied fruit, sugared nuts

34–5 **messengers ... youth** gifts which have a lot of power to influence a young girl

36   **filched** stolen

38   **harshness** hostility

39   **Be it so** if

41   **privilege** special right, law

42   **dispose of her** deal with her, make arrangements for her

45   **Immediately** expressly

46   **Be advised** Consider carefully

49–51 **To whom ... disfigure it** Theseus suggests that a daughter has been created by her father, and, as though she were a wax model, she can either be left in the finished state or be destroyed by him.

EGEUS   Full of vexation come I, with complaint
Against my child, my daughter Hermia.
Stand forth, Demetrius. My noble lord,
This man hath my consent to marry her.   25
Stand forth, Lysander. And my gracious duke,
This man hath bewitched the bosom of my child.
Thou, thou, Lysander, thou hast given her rhymes,
And interchanged love-tokens with my child.
Thou hast by moonlight at her window sung,   30
With feigning voice, verses of feigning love,
And stolen the impression of her fantasy
With bracelets of thy hair, rings, gawds, conceits,
Knacks, trifles, nosegays, sweetmeats –
    messengers
Of strong prevailment in unhardened youth.   35
With cunning hast thou filched my daughter's
    heart,
Turned her obedience, which is due to me,
To stubborn harshness. And, my gracious duke,
Be it so she will not here before your grace
Consent to marry with Demetrius,   40
I beg the ancient privilege of Athens.
As she is mine, I may dispose of her
Which shall be either to this gentleman,
Or to her death, according to our law
Immediately provided in that case.   45

THESEUS   What say you Hermia? Be advised fair maid.
To you your father should be as a god;
One that composed your beauties; yea and one
To whom you are but as a form in wax
By him imprinted, and within his power   50
To leave the figure or disfigure it.
Demetrius is a worthy gentleman.

HERMIA   So is Lysander.

THESEUS   In himself he is,

Hermia insists that she would rather become a nun than marry Demetrius. Theseus gives Hermia until his wedding day to decide.

54	**in this kind** in this respect
	wanting lacking
	voice approval, favour
58	**entreat** beg
65	**die the death** be put to death by the state
	abjure renounce; Hermia's choice, if she will not obey her father, is to be put to death or to spend the rest of her life as a nun.
67–8	**question ... blood** Theseus urges her to think hard about her emotions and her needs and to remember that she is young.
68	**blood** passions
69	**yield** give way
70	**livery** costume, habit
71	**aye** ever
	mewed shut up
73	**fruitless moon** i.e. the moon goddess, Diana, a virgin, the symbol of chastity
74	**master ... blood** control their passions in this way
75	**undergo ... pilgrimage** submit themselves to life as a virgin
76	**earthlier happy** happier on earth
	the rose distilled Perfume was distilled from roses. Theseus is suggesting that a woman who marries is happier than one who gives everything up to become a nun.
80	**patent** privilege
81	**his lordship** Demetrius as my husband
	unwished yoke unwanted domination, marriage
81–2	**whose ... sovereignty** She is saying 'my whole being rejects this marriage. I cannot call him my lord and master.'
84	**sealing-day** wedding-day
88	**as he would** as your father wishes
89	**protest** make a vow

	But in this kind, wanting your father's voice,	
	The other must be held the worthier.	55
HERMIA	I would my father looked but with my eyes.	
THESEUS	Rather your eyes must with his judgement look.	
HERMIA	I do entreat your grace to pardon me.	
	I know not by what power I am made bold,	
	Nor how it may concern my modesty	60
	In such a presence here to plead my thoughts.	
	But I beseech your grace that I may know	
	The worst that may befall me in this case,	
	If I refuse to wed Demetrius.	
THESEUS	Either to die the death, or to abjure	65
	For ever the society of men.	
	Therefore, fair Hermia, question your desires,	
	Know of your youth, examine well your blood,	
	Whether, if you yield not to your father's choice,	
	You can endure the livery of a nun,	70
	For aye to be in shady cloister mewed,	
	To live a barren sister all your life,	
	Chanting faint hymns to the cold fruitless moon.	
	Thrice-blessed they that master so their blood,	
	To undergo such maiden pilgrimage.	75
	But earthlier happy is the rose distilled,	
	Than that which withering on the virgin thorn	
	Grows, lives, and dies in single blessedness.	
HERMIA	So will I grow, so live, so die, my lord,	
	Ere I will yield my virgin patent up	80
	Unto his lordship, whose unwished yoke	
	My soul consents not to give sovereignty.	
THESEUS	Take time to pause, and, by the next new moon –	
	The sealing-day betwixt my love and me,	
	For everlasting bond of fellowship –	85
	Upon that day either prepare to die	
	For disobedience to your father's will,	
	Or else to wed Demetrius, as he would,	
	Or on Diana's altar to protest	

Egeus, Demetrius and Lysander argue the case. Lysander mentions that until recently Demetrius has been in love with Helena. She is still madly in love with him.

90	**for aye austerity** self-discipline for ever
91	**Relent** Change your mind
91–2	**yield ... title** give up your silly claim
96	**render** give
98	**estate** grant to, settle on
99	**I am ... as he** I am from as good a family as he is
100	**As well possessed** owning as much
101	**My fortunes ... ranked** my possessions are equally comparable
102	**with vantage** better
105	**prosecute my right** follow up my claim
106	**avouch ... head** state it to his face
107	**Made ... Helena** told Helena he loved her
108	**soul** heart
108–10	**dotes ... Upon** worships as if he were a god
110	**spotted and inconstant** secondhand and changeable; Lysander is making it clear that Hermia is not Demetrius' first love.
113–14	**being ... lose it** as my mind was chiefly concerned with my own affairs, I forgot
116	**schooling** advice
120	**extenuate** tone down, alter for the better
125	**Against our nuptial** to do with our wedding

For aye austerity and single life.   90

DEMETRIUS Relent, sweet Hermia: and, Lysander, yield
Thy crazed title to my certain right.

LYSANDER You have her father's love, Demetrius;
Let me have Hermia's. Do you marry him.

EGEUS Scornful Lysander, true, he hath my love,   95
And what is mine my love shall render him.
And she is mine, and all my right of her
I do estate unto Demetrius.

LYSANDER I am my lord, as well derived as he,
As well possessed. My love is more than his;   100
My fortunes every way as fairly ranked,
If not with vantage, as Demetrius';
And, which is more than all these boasts can be,
I am beloved of beauteous Hermia.
Why should not I then prosecute my right?   105
Demetrius, I'll avouch it to his head,
Made love to Nedar's daughter, Helena,
And won her soul; and she, sweet lady, dotes,
Devoutly dotes, dotes in idolatry,
Upon this spotted and inconstant man.   110

THESEUS I must confess that I have heard so much,
And with Demetrius thought to have spoke thereof;
But, being over-full of self-affairs,
My mind did lose it. Demetrius come,
And come Egeus, you shall go with me,   115
I have some private schooling for you both.
For you fair Hermia, look you arm yourself
To fit your fancies to your father's will;
Or else the law of Athens yields you up –
Which by no means we may extenuate –   120
To death, or to a vow of single life.
Come my Hippolyta, what cheer my love?
Demetrius and Egeus go along,
I must employ you in some business
Against our nuptial, and confer with you   125

Lysander and Hermia are left alone together. They talk about the pleasure and pain of being in love. Lysander has a plan for their future and starts to tell Hermia about it.

130   **Belike** Perhaps

130–1   **well beteem them** easily allow

131   **from ... eyes** from the storm in my eyes; Hermia is unhappy and near to tears.

132   **For aught** From anything

133   **by tale or history** from talk or from a story

135   **different in blood** The lovers were not of the same social class.

136   **O cross! ... low** What a cross to bear! Of too high a rank to be enslaved to a lower one

137   **misgraffed** badly matched (by age)

139   **stood upon** depended on

141   **sympathy** agreement

142   **lay siege to** lie in wait to attack

143   **momentany** brief

145   **collied** blackened, dark

146   **spleen** The part of the body regarded as producing emotions and passions; (here) fit or flash of anger

147   **ere** before (i.e. before you can say 'Look at the lightning!', it has gone – lost in the darkness again)

149   **So quick ... confusion** so quickly do bright things get destroyed

150   **have ... crossed** have always met with difficulties

151   **It ... destiny** it has the force of a law in our fate

152–3   **Then ... cross** So we must learn to have patience in our difficulties because it is a common hardship

154   **As due to love** as natural to love, as much part of love

155   **fancy's** love's

156   **persuasion** argument

157   **dowager** a widow who has property from her husband

158   **Of great revenue** really very rich

Of something nearly that concerns yourselves.

EGEUS   With duty and desire we follow you.

[Exeunt all but LYSANDER *and* HERMIA

LYSANDER   How now my love? Why is your cheek so pale?
How chance the roses there do fade so fast?

HERMIA   Belike for want of rain, which I could well   130
Beteem them from the tempest of my eyes.

LYSANDER   Ay me! For aught that I could ever read,
Could ever hear by tale or history,
The course of true love never did run smooth;
But either it was different in blood –   135

HERMIA   O cross! Too high to be enthralled to low.

LYSANDER   Or else misgraffed in respect of years –

HERMIA   O spite! Too old to be engaged to young.

LYSANDER   Or else it stood upon the choice of friends –

HERMIA   O hell! To choose love by another's eyes.   140

LYSANDER   Or, if there were a sympathy in choice,
War, death, or sickness did lay siege to it,
Making it momentany as a sound,
Swift as a shadow, short as any dream;
Brief as the lightning in the collied night,   145
That, in a spleen, unfolds both heaven and earth,
And ere a man hath power to say 'Behold!'
The jaws of darkness do devour it up.
So quick bright things come to confusion.

HERMIA   If then true lovers have been ever crossed,   150
It stands as an edict in destiny.
Then let us teach our trial patience,
Because it is a customary cross,
As due to love, as thoughts and dreams and sighs,
Wishes and tears, poor fancy's followers.   155

LYSANDER   A good persuasion. Therefore hear me, Hermia.
I have a widow aunt, a dowager
Of great revenue, and she hath no child;

Hermia and Lysander arrange to meet in the wood the following evening. They have agreed to elope and marry away from Athens and its cruel laws. Helena arrives. She cannot get Demetrius to love her.

159   **seven leagues** about 35 km

164   **Steal forth** creep away from

165   **a league without** 5 km outside

167   **To ... May** to carry out the May Day ceremonies

168   **stay** wait

169   **Cupid's strongest bow** Cupid was the boy-god of love, the son of the goddess Venus. He had wings and a bow and arrows. He was able to make people fall in love by shooting his arrows at them.

171   **Venus'** Venus was the Roman goddess of love. Doves were sacred to her.

173   **Carthage queen** Dido was queen of Carthage and welcomed Aeneas when he escaped from the destruction of Troy. When he left her she took her own life by throwing herself onto her funeral pyre.

174   **the false Troyan** Aeneas had been commanded by Jupiter, the supreme god, to leave Carthage, so he had to go.

175–6   **By all ... spoke** Hermia swears by all the vows ever sworn by men, and broken by them – more than women ever made.

180   **fair** beautiful

       whither away? where are you going?

181   **fair again unsay** cancel that word 'beautiful'

182   **your fair** your style of beauty

       O happy fair! You are lucky in your beauty!

183   **lodestars** guiding-stars

       your ... air the sound of your words

184   **tuneable** tuneful, musical

186   **favour** good looks

190   **bated** excepted

191   **translated** transformed, changed

From Athens is her house remote seven leagues,
And she respects me as her only son.   160
There, gentle Hermia, may I marry thee;
And to that place the sharp Athenian law
Cannot pursue us. If thou lov'st me then,
Steal forth thy father's house tomorrow night,
And in the wood, a league without the town,   165
Where I did meet thee once with Helena,
To do observance to a morn of May,
There will I stay for thee.

HERMIA   My good Lysander,
I swear to thee by Cupid's strongest bow,
By his best arrow with the golden head,   170
By the simplicity of Venus' doves,
By that which knitteth souls, and prospers loves,
And by that fire which burned the Carthage queen,
When the false Troyan under sail was seen,
By all the vows that ever men have broke,   175
In number more than ever women spoke,
In that same place thou hast appointed me,
Tomorrow truly will I meet with thee.

LYSANDER   Keep promise love. Look, here comes Helena.

Enter HELENA

HERMIA   God speed fair Helena, whither away?   180

HELENA   Call you me fair? That fair again unsay.
Demetrius loves your fair. O happy fair!
Your eyes are lode-stars, and your tongue's sweet air
More tuneable than lark to shepherd's ear,
When wheat is green, when hawthorn buds appear. 185
Sickness is catching. O were favour so,
Yours would I catch, fair Hermia, ere I go,
My ear should catch your voice, my eye your eye,
My tongue should catch your tongue's sweet melody.
Were the world mine, Demetrius being bated,   190
The rest I'd give to be to you translated.

The two women have been close childhood friends. Now Helena wants to know why it is Hermia's beauty that attracts Demetrius. Hermia says that she cannot put Demetrius off and she hates him. To comfort Helena Hermia tells her that she is leaving with Lysander and they plan to elope.

192	**art** skill
193	**sway the motion** influence the beating
200	**folly** foolishness
201	**would** I wish
203	**fly** run away from
206	**what ... dwell** what charming qualities are present in the man I love
208	**our minds ... unfold** we will tell you what we mean to do
209	**Phoebe** the moon; according to Greek **myth** (see Glossary p. 227) Phoebe is the daughter of Uranus (Heaven) and Gaia (Earth). Her name was later used to mean the moon.
210	**Her ... glass** The shining moon is reflected in a pool.
	visage face
211	**Decking ... pearl** making the dewdrops on the grass look like pearls
212	**still** always
213	**Through ... steal** we have thought of a way of slipping through the town gates
215	**faint** pale
	were wont to used to
216	**Emptying ... sweet** having a heart-to-heart, telling each other our most secret thoughts
218	**thence** from there
219	**stranger companies** fresh companions
222–3	**we must ... midnight** we won't be able to see each other again until midnight tomorrow

O teach me how you look, and with what art
You sway the motion of Demetrius' heart.

HERMIA   I frown upon him, yet he loves me still.

HELENA   O that your frowns would teach my smiles such
skill.   195

HERMIA   I give him curses, yet he gives me love.

HELENA   O that my prayers could such affection move.

HERMIA   The more I hate, the more he follows me.

HELENA   The more I love, the more he hateth me.

HERMIA   His folly, Helena, is no fault of mine.   200

HELENA   None but your beauty; would that fault were mine.

HERMIA   Take comfort. He no more shall see my face,
Lysander and myself will fly this place.
Before the time I did Lysander see,
Seemed Athens as a paradise to me.   205
O then, what graccs in my love do dwell,
That he hath turned a heaven unto a hell.

LYSANDER Helen, to you our minds we will unfold
Tomorrow night, when Phoebe doth behold
Her silver visage in the watery glass,   210
Decking with liquid pearl the bladed grass –
A time that lovers' flights doth still conceal –
Through Athens' gates have we devised to steal.

HERMIA   And in the wood, where often you and I
Upon faint primrose-beds were wont to lie,   215
Emptying our bosoms of their counsel sweet,
There my Lysander and myself shall meet;
And thence from Athens turn away our eyes
To seek new friends and stranger companies.
Farewell, sweet playfellow; pray thou for us,   220
And good luck grant thee thy Demetrius.
Keep word Lysander, we must starve our sight
From lovers' food, till morrow deep midnight.

LYSANDER I will my Hermia.

[*Exit* HERMIA

41

When she is on her own Helena talks of her deep unhappiness. Demetrius had loved her until he saw Hermia. She decides to tell him of the planned elopement. If this doesn't earn her Demetrius' thanks at least she'll see him in the wood.

225	**As you ... on you** May Demetrius be as deeply in love with you as you are with him
226	**o'er other some** over some others i.e. How much happier some people can be than others!
229	**will not know** refuses to recognise
230	**errs** goes astray, makes mistakes
	doting on foolishly in love with
231	**So I ... qualities** and I am just as mistaken in admiring his character
232	**base and vile** low and mean
	holding no quantity badly proportioned
233	**transpose** change, transform
	form and dignity beauty and worth i.e. Looked at with love, even things that are low, mean and out of proportion will appear full of beauty and worth.
234	**Love ... mind** Love does not depend on what it can actually see, but on what it imagines
235	**therefore ... blind** that is why Cupid is shown with his eyes blindfolded
236	**Nor ... taste** Neither does love's mind have even the least amount of judgement
237	**Wings ... haste** wings and lack of sight suggest speed without thought
240–1	**As waggish ... everywhere** In the same way that, in fun, playful boys will pretend things that are not true, the boy who symbolises love makes false promises too
242	**eyne** eyes
243	**hailed down oaths** sent down a hailstorm of vows
244–5	**when ... melt** when Hermia responded to his declaration of love, his hail-showers of vows melted and so did he
248	**intelligence** information
249	**a dear expense** worth the trouble
250–1	**But herein ... again** I will add to my torment by at least seeing Demetrius on the way to the wood and back again

Helena adieu.

As you on him, Demetrius dote on you.   225

[*Exit* LYSANDER

HELENA How happy some o'er other some can be!
Through Athens I am thought as fair as she.
But what of that? Demetrius thinks not so.
He will not know what all but he do know;
And as he errs, doting on Hermia's eyes,   230
So I, admiring of his qualities.
Things base and vile, holding no quantity,
Love can transpose to form and dignity.
Love looks not with the eyes, but with the mind,
And therefore is winged Cupid painted blind.   235
Nor hath Love's mind of any judgement taste;
Wings and no eyes figure unheedy haste.
And therefore is Love said to be a child,
Because in choice he is so oft beguiled.
As waggish boys in game themselves forswear,   240
So the boy Love is perjured everwhere.
For ere Demetrius looked on Hermia's eyne,
He hailed down oaths that he was only mine;
And when this hail some heat from Hermia felt,
So he dissolved, and showers of oaths did melt.   245
I will go tell him of fair Hermia's flight.
Then to the wood will he tomorrow night
Pursue her; and for this intelligence
If I have thanks, it is a dear expense.
But herein mean I to enrich my pain,   250
To have his sight thither and back again.

[*Exit*

The Athenian workmen who will act in a play for the royal wedding celebrations have been chosen. They meet to be given their parts. Quince, the carpenter, is in charge.

SD   The meanings sometimes suggested for the workmen's names are as follows: Quince from 'quoin', a wedge used in carpentry; Snug from the tight joints made by a good joiner; Bottom from the ball of thread used by a weaver; Flute for the bellows-mender suggests the high sound of an organ pipe; Snout, the tinker, possibly from the shape of a kettle's spout; Starveling because tailors were renowned for being poor.

2   **generally** Bottom's mistake for the word meaning 'individually'.

3   **scrip** piece of paper with writing on it; (here) what you've got written down

4   **scroll** list

6   **interlude** play

8   **treats on** is about, deals with

10   **grow to a point** get to the main business

11   **Marry** Indeed

12   **Pyramus and Thisby** Originally a story in Ovid's *Metamorphoses* which Chaucer also made use of. Two young people in love lived next door to each other. As their parents would not let them marry, they used to talk through a hole in the wall. They managed to arrange a meeting, but a lion's roar frightened Thisby away. As she ran she dropped her cloak. When Pyramus arrived and saw it, he thought she must be dead. He stabbed himself. When Thisby returned and saw that he was dead, she killed herself also.

15   **Masters** A form of address: 'Gentlemen'

        spread yourselves spread out

23   **condole** lament, express grief

25   **Ercles** Hercules, famous in Greek mythology for his great strength and cleverness.

        a part ... cat in a part needing violent action and loud, ranting speeches

26   **all split** a terrific, ear-splitting row

Scene ❷

Peter Quince's house

Enter, QUINCE, SNUG, BOTTOM, FLUTE, SNOUT, *and*
STARVELING

QUINCE   Is all our company here?

BOTTOM   You were best to call them generally, man by
man, according to the scrip.

QUINCE   Here is the scroll of every man's name, which is
thought fit, through all Athens, to play in our   5
interlude before the duke and the duchess, on his
wedding-day at night.

BOTTOM   First good Peter Quince, say what the play treats
on, then read the names of the actors, and so
grow to a point.   10

QUINCE   Marry, our play is, 'The most lamentable comedy,
and most cruel death of Pyramus and Thisby'.

BOTTOM   A very good piece of work I assure you, and a
merry. Now, good Peter Quince, call forth your
actors by the scroll. Masters, spread yourselves.   15

QUINCE   Answer as I call you. Nick Bottom the weaver.

BOTTOM   Ready. Name what part I am for, and proceed.

QUINCE   You, Nick Bottom, are set down for Pyramus.

BOTTOM   What is Pyramus? A lover, or a tyrant?

QUINCE   A lover that kills himself most gallant for love.   20

BOTTOM   That will ask some tears in the true performing of
it. If I do it, let the audience look to their eyes; I
will move storms, I will condole in some measure.
To the rest. Yet my chief humour is for a tyrant; I
could play Ercles rarely, or a part to tear a cat in,   25
to make all split.

Bottom, the weaver, is the dominant personality and can see himself in every role.

31   **Phibbus' car** the chariot of Phoebus, the sun-god

34   **The Fates** Three goddesses with influence over the life and death of men and women. The first was there at the birth, the second spun out the events of his/her life and at the end the third cut the thread of life.

36   **Ercles' vein** the way Hercules would do it

37   **condoling** moving

45   **That's all one** That doesn't matter

46   **as small ... will** in as tiny, high a voice as you want

47   **An** If

48   **monstrous little** amazingly small (as Bottom immediately demonstrates)

The raging rocks
And shivering shocks
Shall break the locks
 Of prison-gates; 30
And Phibbus' car
Shall shine from far,
And make and mar
 The foolish Fates.

This was lofty. Now name the rest of the players. 35
This is Ercles' vein, a tyrant's vein. A lover is
more condoling.

QUINCE Francis Flute the bellows-mender.

FLUTE Here Peter Quince.

QUINCE Flute, you must take Thisby on you. 40

FLUTE What is Thisby? A wandering knight?

QUINCE It is the lady that Pyramus must love.

FLUTE Nay faith, let not me play a woman, I have a
beard coming.

QUINCE That's all one. You shall play it in a mask, and 45
you may speak as small as you will.

BOTTOM An I may hide my face, let me play Thisby too.
I'll speak in a monstrous little voice, 'Thisne,
Thisne'. 'Ah Pyramus, my lover dear, Thy Thisby
dear, and lady dear.' 50

QUINCE No no; you must play Pyramus, and Flute, you
Thisby.

BOTTOM Well, proceed.

QUINCE Robin Starveling the tailor.

STARVELING Here Peter Quince. 55

QUINCE Robin Starveling, you must play Thisby's mother.
Tom Snout the tinker.

SNOUT Here Peter Quince.

QUINCE You, Pyramus' father; myself, Thisby's father;
Snug the joiner, you the lion's part. And, I hope, 60

Bottom continues to dominate the discussion, offering a variety of make-up for his part.

61	**fitted** cast
62–3	**if it be** if it is (already written down)
64	**extempore** without a script, whenever it seems to fit in
70	**An ... do it** If you were to do it
72	**were** would be
76	**aggravate** make worse (Bottom means 'make quieter'.)
78	**sucking dove** Doves are birds and they don't suck milk; they have beaks.
78–9	**I will ... nightingale** I'll roar as loudly as if I were a nightingale (Nightingales do sing loudly.)
80	**You can ... Pyramus** You must act Pyramus and nothing else
81	**sweet-faced** good-looking
	proper handsome
83	**must needs** absolutely have to
86	**what you will** whatever you like
88	**orange-tawny** dull yellowy-brown
88–9	**purple-in-grain** deep-dyed red
89	**French-crown-colour** the golden colour of the French 'crown' coin
91	**Some ... at all** Some French heads are bald (This could be the result of syphilis, known then as 'the French disease'.)
93–4	**entreat ... request ... desire** Three ways of saying 'please' to stress the importance of learning their parts.
94	**con** learn by heart
95	**the palace wood** Duke Theseus' forest

	here is a play fitted.
SNUG	Have you the lion's part written? Pray you, if it be, give it me, for I am slow of study.
QUINCE	You may do it extempore, for it is nothing but roaring.

65

| BOTTOM | Let me play the lion too. I will roar, that I will do any man's heart good to hear me. I will roar, that I will make the duke say, 'Let him roar again, let him roar again.' |

| QUINCE | An you should do it too terribly, you would fright the duchess and the ladies, that they would shriek, and that were enough to hang us all. |

70

| ALL | That would hang us, every mother's son. |

| BOTTOM | I grant you, friends, if you should fright the ladies out of their wits, they would have no more discretion but to hang us; but I will aggravate my voice so, that I will roar you as gently as any sucking dove; I will roar you an 'twere any nightingale. |

75

| QUINCE | You can play no part but Pyramus, for Pyramus is a sweet-faced man, a proper man as one shall see in a summer's day; a most lovely, gentleman-like man therefore you must needs play Pyramus. |

80

| BOTTOM | Well, I will undertake it. What beard were I best to play it in? |

85

| QUINCE | Why, what you will. |

| BOTTOM | I will discharge it in either your straw-colour beard, your orange-tawny beard, your purple-in-grain beard, or your French-crown-colour beard, your perfect yellow. |

90

| QUINCE | Some of your French crowns have no hair at all, and then you will play barefaced. But masters, here are your parts, and I am to entreat you, request you, and desire you, to con them by tomorrow night; and meet me in the palace wood, |

95

They arrange a rehearsal in the wood for the following evening.

96   **without** outside

97–8   **we shall … company** people will come and watch us

98   **our devices known** they'll know what we're doing

99–100 **draw … wants** make a list of stage properties needed for the play

100   **fail me not** don't forget to come

102   **obscenely** Bottom might mean 'seemly' – properly, or more likely 'obscurely' since they obviously want to rehearse in secret.

102–3   **be perfect** make sure you are word perfect

105   **Hold … bow-strings** Stand firm, stay with it, or call it a day. 'Cut bow-strings' is obscure but it is possible that long-bow archers when overcome in battle would make their weapon useless to the other side by cutting the bow-string.

a mile without the town, by moonlight; there will
we rehearse. For if we meet in the city, we shall be
dogged with company, and our devices known. In
the meantime I will draw a bill of properties, such
as our play wants. I pray you, fail me not.   100

BOTTOM   We will meet, and there we may rehearse most
            obscenely and courageously. Take pains, be
            perfect. Adieu.

QUINCE   At the duke's oak we meet.

BOTTOM   Enough. Hold or cut bow-strings.   105

                                                 [*Exeunt*

Act 1 scenes 1 and 2

The love tangle

It's easy to become confused about who loves whom and who rejects whom in this play. What's more, as the play develops, things become even more complicated. So it's a good idea to get a firm grip on the situation at the beginning of the play.

In scene 1, we meet these characters:

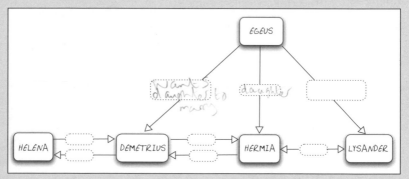

As you can see, on each arrow there is an empty box. The missing words for each box are:

- daughter
- does not want daughter to marry
- loves
- loves
- loves
- rejects
- rejects
- wants daughter to marry.

Work with a partner

1 Copy out the diagram onto a large sheet of paper.

2 Read through scene 1 and work out which word(s) should go in each box.

3 Write them in.

Plot lines

Act 1 introduces three different plots:

- **Theseus and Hippolyta** are preparing for their wedding.
- **The young lovers** are in a tangle and Egeus is acting the heavy-handed father.
- **Bottom and his friends** are planning an entertainment for the wedding of Theseus and Hippolyta.

We can set out these separate plots in a table, like this:

Plot line 1: **Theseus and Hippolyta**	Plot line 2: **The young lovers**	Plot line 3: **Bottom and his friends**	Plot line 4: **Oberon and Titania**
Theseus has won Hippolyta in battle.	Egeus says that Hermia must marry Demetrius or die.	Quince and the actors meet in the woods to plan their play.	

(The fourth column contains characters we haven't met yet.)

Here are some more plot points:

- Quince is the director of the play.
- Helena is sad that she loves Demetrius but he loves Hermia, not her.
- Quince gives out the scripts.
- The Duke supports Egeus.
- Lysander and Hermia declare their love for each other. They plan to elope.
- Hermia says she loves Lysander.
- They are to be married in four days' time, with great festivities.
- Bottom wants to play all the parts, but has to settle for Pyramus.
- Helena says she'll tell Demetrius what Hermia and Lysander are planning.

Work with a partner

1 Copy out the table. You will need five more rows of boxes.
2 Put each of the plot points in the right box.
   Warning: the list is not in the right order!

Love and marriage

A Midsummer Night's Dream explores people's ideas about love and marriage. This begins in the very first scene. We can examine this by setting different characters' ideas out in a table:

	Point	Evidence	Explanation
Theseus	Believes that men are superior to women and that love between them is like a battle.	'I wooed thee with my sword, And won thy love doing thee injuries.'	He literally won Hippolyta in battle, but he also believes that he should continue to dominate her in marriage.
Demetrius			
Egeus			
Helena			
Hermia			
Lysander			

Work with a partner

1 Copy out the table. As you can see, it has been started for you.

2 Decide what attitude each of the characters has towards love and/ or marriage. Write it in the 'Point' column.

3 Now find a quotation from scene 1 which supports each point you have made. Write that in the 'Evidence' column.

4 For each piece of evidence explain why it supports the point you have made. Write your explanation in the right-hand column.

5 Prepare a short presentation for the rest of the class on this topic: *What do we learn about attitudes towards love and marriage from Act 1 scene 1?*

Quotation quiz

For each of these quotations, work out:

1 who said it
2 who they were speaking to
3 what it tells us about
   a the speaker
   b the situation
   c any other characters.

A
How now my love? Why is your cheek so pale?
How chance the roses there do fade so fast?

B
…our nuptial hour
Draws on apace.

C
…yield
Thy crazed title to my right.

D
Let me play the lion too. I will roar, that I will do any man's heart good to hear me.

E
In that same place thou hast appointed me,
Tomorrow truly will I meet with thee.

F
Nay faith, let me not play a woman, I have a beard coming.

G
Full of vexation come I, with complaint
Against my child…

H
We will meet, and there we may rehearse most obscenely and courageously.

I
I give him curses, yet he gives me love.

J
The more I love, the more he hateth me.

Puck, who serves Oberon, the Fairy King, and a fairy who serves Titania, the Fairy Queen, meet. Puck explains that Oberon will be in the wood that evening and that he and Titania have quarrelled over the ownership of a human child.

SD	**PUCK** A devil or imp also known as Robin Goodfellow. This was a safe way of referring to Puck who does such annoying things. If he is a 'good fellow' he is less likely to do you harm, and might even help you.
1	**whither wander you?** where are you going?
3	**Thorough** through
4	**pale** fence
7	**moon's sphere** the orbit of the moon
9	**To dew** to water
	orbs Fairy rings, circles of darker grass, believed to be where fairies danced.
10	**pensioners** Bodyguards to the king or queen within the royal palace, first set up by Henry VIII, and chosen for their height.
12	**favours** gifts
13	**savours** smells, perfumes
16	**lob** clown, lout
17	**elves** young boy fairies
	anon soon, shortly
18	**doth ... revels** holds his entertainments
19	**Take heed** Take care
20	**passing fell** exceedingly angry
	wrath furious
23	**a changeling** Usually a child left by fairies in exchange for a human child they had stolen; (here) the stolen child
25	**train** followers, attendants
	trace range over, pass through
26	**perforce** by force

Act Two

Scene ❶

A wood near Athens

Enter a FAIRY *at one door, and* PUCK *at another*

PUCK	How now, spirit, whither wander you?
FAIRY	Over hill, over dale,

Thorough bush, thorough brier,
Over park, over pale,
Thorough flood, thorough fire;   5
I do wander every where,
Swifter than the moon's sphere;
And I serve the Fairy Queen,
To dew her orbs upon the green.
The cowslips tall her pensioners be,   10
In their gold coats spots you see,
Those be rubies, fairy favours,
In those freckles live their savours.
I must go seek some dewdrops here,
And hang a pearl in every cowslip's ear.   15
Farewell thou lob of spirits; I'll be gone.
Our queen and all her elves come here anon.

PUCK   The king doth keep his revels here tonight.
Take heed the queen come not within his sight.
For Oberon is passing fell and wrath,   20
Because that she, as her attendant, hath
A lovely boy stolen from an Indian king.
She never had so sweet a changeling.
And jealous Oberon would have the child
Knight of his train, to trace the forests wild.   25
But she perforce witholds the loved boy,
Crowns him with flowers, and makes him all her joy.
And now they never meet in grove, or green,

The fairy recognises Puck as the imp who plays tricks on humans and amuses his master. Puck describes some of his favourite tricks. Oberon and Titania meet. Titania makes it clear she does not want to see him, or be with him.

29	**starlight sheen** shining light of the stars
30	**square** quarrel
31	**acorn-cups** The small cup-shaped holders of acorns on oak trees.
32	**making** build, form
33	**shrewd** mischievous
34	**Robin Goodfellow** Another name for Puck.
35	**villagery** villages
36	**Skim milk** steal the cream
	quern A hand-mill for grinding corn.
37	**bootless** uselessly (Puck stops the milk being churned into butter.)
38	**barm** froth on beer
40	**Hobgoblin** Another name for Robin Goodfellow or Puck.
45	**beguile** trick
47	**gossip** old woman
48	**crab** crab apple
50	**dewlap** loose skin hanging from the neck
51	**aunt** old woman
	saddest most serious
54	**'tailor'** tail! bum! (an exclamation used when someone sits down heavily on the floor)
	falls ... cough has a coughing fit
55	**choir** company
56	**waxen ... mirth** their laughter increases
	neeze sneeze
57	**wasted** spent
58	**room** draw back, make way
59	**Would ... gone** I wish he were not here
60	**Ill met** An unfortunate meeting
61	**hence** away
62	**I have ... company** I have sworn not to share his bed or his company

	By fountain clear, or spangled starlight sheen,
	But they do square, that all their elves for fear	30
	Creep into acorn-cups and hide them there.
FAIRY	Either I mistake your shape and making quite,
	Or else you are that shrewd and knavish sprite
	Called Robin Goodfellow. Are not you he,
	That frights the maidens of the villagery,	35
	Skim milk, and sometime labour in the quern,
	And bootless make the breathless housewife churn,
	And sometime make the drink to bear no barm,
	Mislead night-wanderers, laughing at their harm?
	Those that Hobgoblin call you, and sweet Puck,	40
	You do their work, and they shall have good luck.
	Are not you he?
PUCK	Thou speak'st aright;
	I am that merry wanderer of the night.
	I jest to Oberon and make him smile,
	When I a fat and bean-fed horse beguile,	45
	Neighing in likeness of a filly foal;
	And sometimes lurk I in a gossip's bowl,
	In very likeness of a roasted crab,
	And when she drinks, against her lips I bob,
	And on her withered dewlap pour the ale.	50
	The wisest aunt, telling the saddest tale,
	Sometime for three-foot stool mistaketh me;
	Then slip I from her bum, down topples she,
	And 'tailor' cries, and falls into a cough;
	And then the whole choir hold their hips and laugh,	55
	And waxen in their mirth, and neeze, and swear
	A merrier hour was never wasted there.
	But room, fairy, here comes Oberon.
FAIRY	And here my mistress. Would that he were gone.
	Enter OBERON *at one door, with his train; and*
	TITANIA *at another, with hers*
OBERON	Ill met by moonlight, proud Titania.	60
TITANIA	What, jealous Oberon? Fairies, skip hence.
	I have forsworn his bed and company.

Titania and Oberon accuse one another of having been in love with
Hippolyta and Theseus. Their quarrels have caused unseasonal weather.

63	**Tarry, rash wanton** Wait hasty mistress
64–5	**I know ... away** I have seen you creep away
66–8	**in ... Phillida** disguised as a shepherd, you have sat playing on pipes of straw and singing love songs to Phillida
69	**step** limit
70	**But that, forsooth** Only because, indeed
	the bouncing Amazon that strapping wench (Hippolyta)
71	**Your buskined mistress** your lady of the hunting boots
	warrior soldier; Hippolyta, was Queen of the Amazons. Theseus defeated them in battle and married her.
73	**their bed ... prosperity** their life together happiness and success
74	**How ... shame** You should be really ashamed
75	**Glance ... credit** throw doubt on my reputation
77	**glimmering night** night just as dawn begins to show
78–80	**From ... Antopia** Oberon claims Titania has made Theseus desert at least three women.
78	**ravished** carried off
81	**forgeries** false inventions
82	**middle summer's spring** the beginning of midsummer
83	**dale** valley
	mead meadow
85	**beached margent** shingle sea-shore
86	**ringlets** circular dances
87	**sport** pleasure
90	**Contagious** harmful
91–2	**Have ... continents** all the little rivers have swollen and burst their banks
94–5	**The ploughman ... beard** the ploughman's work was pointless as the barley plants have rotted before producing grain (When ripe each grain looks to have a beard.)
97	**murrion flock** diseased sheep
98	**nine men's morris** An area marked out for an outdoor game, something like draughts. Each player had nine pieces.

OBERON	Tarry, rash wanton. Am not I thy lord?	
TITANIA	Then I must be thy lady. But I know	
	When thou hast stolen away from fairy land,	65
	And in the shape of Corin sat all day,	
	Playing on pipes of corn, and versing love	
	To amorous Phillida. Why art thou here,	
	Come from the farthest step of India?	
	But that, forsooth, the bouncing Amazon,	70
	Your buskined mistress, and your warrior love,	
	To Theseus must be wedded; and you come	
	To give their bed joy and prosperity.	
OBERON	How canst thou thus for shame, Titania,	
	Glance at my credit with Hippolyta,	75
	Knowing I know thy love to Theseus?	
	Didst thou not lead him through the glimmering	
	night	
	From Peregenia, whom he ravished?	
	And make him with fair Ægles break his faith,	
	With Ariadne, and Antiopa?	80
TITANIA	These are the forgeries of jealousy.	
	And never, since the middle summer's spring,	
	Met we on hill, in dale, forest, or mead,	
	By paved fountain, or by rushy brook,	
	Or in the beached margent of the sea,	85
	To dance our ringlets to the whistling wind,	
	But with thy brawls thou hast disturbed our sport.	
	Therefore the winds, piping to us in vain,	
	As in revenge, have sucked up from the sea	
	Contagious fogs; which falling in the land,	90
	Have every pelting river made so proud,	
	That they have overborne their continents.	
	The ox hath therefore stretched his yoke in vain,	
	The ploughman lost his sweat, and the green corn	
	Hath rotted ere his youth attained a beard.	95
	The fold stands empty in the drowned field,	
	And crows are fatted with the murrion flock;	
	The nine men's morris is filled up with mud,	

Titania reminds Oberon that the disastrous climate changes are the result of their quarrels. He tells her she can put it right by handing over the child. She refuses.

99   **quaint mazes** Complicated pattern of paths, often used, and so usually easy to see.

      wanton green luxuriant grass

101   **want ... cheer** lack their winter entertainments

103   **governess** controller

106   **distemperature** 1) bad temper 2) bad weather

107   **hoary** greyish-white

109   **Hiems** Winter is **personified** (see Glossary p. 228).

      crown head

110   **odorous chaplet** sweet-smelling garland

112   **childing** fertile, fruitful

113   **wonted liveries** usual clothes

      mazed bewildered, confused

114   **increase** seasonal produce; in the changed weather you cannot tell by looking at the produce which season is which.

115   **progeny of evils** family of disasters

115–16 **comes ... dissension** is the result of our quarrel, our disagreement

117   **original** origin

118   **Do you amend it** Put it right

      it lies in you you have the power

121   **henchman** page

123   **vot'ress** votaress (i.e. a woman who has taken a vow); she was a member of Titania's order.

126   **Neptune** god of water

127   **Marking ... flood** watching the merchant ships passing on the sea

128–34 **When ... merchandise** Titania and her pregnant friend used to laugh, comparing the ship's round sails with her pregnant figure. She would pretend to be a ship and bring gifts to Titania as if from her cargo. Her child is now Titania's page.

And the quaint mazes in the wanton green,
For lack of tread, are undistinguishable.   100
The human mortals want their winter cheer,
No night is now with hymn or carol blest.
Therefore the moon, the governess of floods,
Pale in her anger, washes all the air,
That rheumatic diseases do abound.   105
And thorough this distemperature we see
The seasons alter; hoary-headed frosts
Fall in the fresh lap of the crimson rose,
And on old Hiems' thin and icy crown
An odorous chaplet of sweet summer buds   110
Is, as in mockery, set. The spring, the summer,
The childing autumn, angry winter, change
Their wonted liveries; and the mazed world,
By their increase, now knows not which is which.
And this same progeny of evils comes   115
From our debate, from our dissension;
We are their parents and original.

OBERON   Do you amend it then, it lies in you.
            Why should Titania cross her Oberon?
            I do but beg a little changeling boy   120
            To be my henchman.

TITANIA   Set your heart at rest,
            The fairy land buys not the child of me.
            His mother was a vot'ress of my order,
            And in the spiced Indian air, by night,
            Full often hath she gossiped by my side,   125
            And sat with me on Neptune's yellow sands,
            Marking th' embarked traders on the flood;
            When we have laughed to see the sails conceive,
            And grow big-bellied with the wanton wind;
            Which she, with pretty and with swimming gait   130
            Following, her womb then rich with my young
                squire,
            Would imitate, and sail upon the land,
            To fetch me trifles, and return again,
            As from a voyage, rich with merchandise.

The boy's mother died in childbirth and because they had been so close, Titania took the child and is bringing him up. She will not part with him. When Titania leaves to avoid a worse quarrel, Oberon vows to torment her. He reminds Puck of a time when they saw an arrow from Cupid's bow fall on a flower.

135	**But she … die**	She, being human, died in childbirth
139	**Perchance**	Perhaps
140	**our round**	our round dance
141	**revels**	celebrations
142	**If not … haunts**	if not, keep away from me and I won't go near you
145	**chide downright**	have a proper fight
146	**Thou … grove**	I won't let you leave this wood
147	**injury**	insult
148	**gentle**	kind
	hither	here (to me)
149	**Since**	when
	promontory	headland
151	**Uttering … breath**	singing such sweet songs
152	**rude**	rough
	civil	calm
153	**certain … spheres**	some stars fell from their appointed place (to get closer to the music)
158	**fair vestal**	beautiful virgin (usually taken to refer to Queen Elizabeth I)
159	**love-shaft**	Cupid's golden arrow
160	**As it**	as if it
162	**Quenched … moon**	Moonbeams put out the blazing arrow. Diana, virgin moon-goddess, was protecting a virgin.
164	**In maiden … fancy-free**	with innocent thoughts, free of love
165	**Yet … fell**	But I noticed where Cupid's arrow fell
167	**Before … wound**	The colour of the flower was changed by contact with Cupid's arrow from innocent white to blood-coloured.

	But she, being mortal, of that boy did die,	135
	And for her sake do I rear up her boy,	
	And for her sake I will not part with him.	
OBERON	How long within this wood intend you stay?	
TITANIA	Perchance till after Theseus' wedding-day.	
	If you will patiently dance in our round,	140
	And see our moonlight revels, go with us;	
	If not, shun me, and I will spare your haunts.	
OBERON	Give me that boy, and I will go with thee.	
TITANIA	Not for thy fairy kingdom. Fairies away,	
	We shall chide downright, if I longer stay.	145

[*Exit* TITANIA *with her train*

OBERON	Well, go thy way. Thou shalt not from this grove.	
	Till I torment thee for this injury.	
	My gentle Puck come hither. Thou remembrest	
	Since once I sat upon a promontory,	
	And heard a mermaid, on a dolphin's back,	150
	Uttering such dulcet and harmonious breath,	
	That the rude sea grew civil at her song,	
	And certain stars shot madly from their spheres,	
	To hear the sea-maid's music.	
PUCK	I remember.	
OBERON	That very time I saw – but thou couldst not –	155
	Flying between the cold moon and the earth,	
	Cupid all armed. A certain aim he took	
	At a fair vestal, throned by the west,	
	And loosed his love-shaft smartly from his bow,	
	As it should pierce a hundred thousand hearts:	160
	But I might see young Cupid's fiery shaft	
	Quenched in the chaste beams of the watery moon,	
	And the imperial vot'ress passed on,	
	In maiden meditation, fancy-free.	
	Yet marked I where the bolt of Cupid fell.	165
	It fell upon a little western flower,	
	Before, milk-white; now purple with love's wound,	

Oberon tells Puck to go and find the flower that had been hit by Cupid's arrow. The juice of it acts as a charm. It will cause the person on whose eyelids it is squeezed to fall madly in love with the first live creature they see upon waking. Oberon is planning to torment Titania and blackmail her into giving up the child. He remains invisible and watches Demetrius and Helena. Demetrius is looking for Lysander in order to kill him. She is pursuing him and begging for his love.

168   **love-in-idleness** pansy or heart's ease

171–2 **or man ... dote** will make either a man or a woman infatuated

172   **Upon ... sees** with whatever live creature he or she sees next

173–4 **Fetch ... league** Bring me this herb and be back here before a whale can swim 5 km

174   **leviathan** sea-monster, whale

175   **put ... earth** make a circuit of the world

176   **Having once** Once I've got

178   **liquor** juice

180   **Be it** whether it is

182   **pursue ... love** go after it with her heart full of love

185   **render up** part with

187   **conference** conversation

191   **were stolen** had come secretly

192   **and wood ... wood** and wildly angry in this wood. This **play on words** was possible in the language of Shakespeare's time (see Glossary p. 228).

195   **adamant** Imaginary stone or very hard mineral, supposed to act like a magnet.

197–8 **Leave you ... follow you** If you give up your power to attract me I shall not be able to follow you

And maidens call it, love-in-idleness.
Fetch me that flower; the herb I showed thee once.
The juice of it on sleeping eyelids laid,   170
Will make or man or woman madly dote
Upon the next live creature that it sees.
Fetch me this herb, and be thou here again
Ere the leviathan can swim a league.

PUCK   I'll put a girdle round about the earth   175
In forty minutes.

[Exit

OBERON   Having once this juice,
I'll watch Titania when she is asleep,
And drop the liquor of it in her eyes.
The next thing then she waking looks upon,
Be it on lion, bear, or wolf, or bull,   180
On meddling monkey or on busy ape,
She shall pursue it with the soul of love.
And ere I take this charm from off her sight –
As I can take it with another herb –
I'll make her render up her page to me.   185
But who comes here? I am invisible,
And I will overhear their conference.

Enter DEMETRIUS, HELENA *following him*

DEMETRIUS I love thee not, therefore pursue me not.
Where is Lysander, and fair Hermia?
The one I'll slay, the other slayeth me.   190
Thou told'st me they were stolen unto this wood;
And here am I, and wood within this wood,
Because I cannot meet my Hermia.
Hence, get thee gone, and follow me no more.

HELENA   You draw me, you hard-hearted adamant;   195
But yet you draw not iron, for my heart
Is true as steel. Leave you your power to draw,
And I shall have no power to follow you.

Demetrius is angry. He has had enough of being followed around by
Helena. She just cannot leave him alone. He points out that she is risking
everything, alone at night in the forest. Nothing he says or does can get rid
of her.

199   **Do I ... fair?** Do I ever tempt you, speak kindly to you?

204   **fawn** Show devotion to a human by crawling and rubbing
against their legs (as a dog would)

205   **spurn me, strike me** kick me, hit me

206   **give me leave** permit me

211   **Tempt ... spirit** Don't go on trying my capacity for hatred too
long

214   **impeach** discredit

214–19 **You ... virginity** You call into question your modesty by leaving
the city and putting yourself in the hands of someone who
doesn't love you; by trusting your virginity, which is so precious,
to the possibilities offered by night and the evil influence of a
lonely place

220   **Your ... privilege** It is your good qualities which make my
circumstance favourable

220–1   **For that ... face** Because it isn't dark when I can look at your
face

224   **in my respect** to my mind

227   **brakes** bushes

230   **Run ... will** Run away whenever you like

231   **Apollo ... chase** Daphne, running away from Apollo, was
changed into a laurel bush to escape from him.

232   **griffin** A legendary animal, half lion, half eagle.

        mild hind gentle doe

233   **Bootless** Pointless

234   **valour** bravery

DEMETRIUS   Do I entice you? Do I speak you fair?
            Or rather do I not in plainest truth   200
            Tell you I do not, nor I cannot love you?

HELENA   And even for that do I love you the more.
            I am your spaniel; and, Demetrius,
            The more you beat me I will fawn on you.
            Use me but as your spaniel, spurn me, strike me,   205
            Neglect me, lose me; only give me leave,
            Unworthy as I am, to follow you.
            What worser place can I beg in your love –
            And yet a place of high respect with me –
            Than to be used as you use your dog?   210

DEMETRIUS   Tempt not too much the hatred of my spirit,
            For I am sick when I do look on thee.

HELENA   And I am sick when I look not on you.

DEMETRIUS   You do impeach your modesty too much,
            To leave the city, and commit yourself   215
            Into the hands of one that loves you not,
            To trust the opportunity of night,
            And the ill counsel of a desert place,
            With the rich worth of your virginity.

HELENA   Your virtue is my privilege. For that   220
            It is not night when I do see your face,
            Therefore I think I am not in the night;
            Nor doth this wood lack worlds of company,
            For you in my respect are all the world.
            Then how can it be said I am alone,   225
            When all the world is here to look on me?

DEMETRIUS   I'll run from thee, and hide me in the brakes,
            And leave thee to the mercy of wild beasts.

HELENA   The wildest hath not such a heart as you.
            Run when you will. The story shall be changed: 230
            Apollo flies, and Daphne holds the chase;
            The dove pursues the griffin; the mild hind
            Makes speed to catch the tiger. Bootless speed,
            When cowardice pursues, and valour flies.

Demetrius goes off, threatening to harm Helena if she persists in following him. She does go after him however. When Puck returns with the flower, Oberon takes it for Titania. Oberon has taken pity on Helena and tells Puck to put some on the eyelids of her young man.

235   **stay** wait for

236–7   **do not ... mischief** you'd better understand that I shall do you harm

238   **temple** church

239   **Fie** An exclamation of disgust.

240   **Your ... sex** the wrongs you do me are making me act in a way that disgraces my sex

242   **We should ... woo** We should be gently tempted into love, it is not in our nature to do the persuading ourselves

244   **die ... hand** be killed by the man

245   **nymph** beautiful young woman

245–6   **Ere ... love** Before he leaves this wood you'll be the one running away and he will want your love

250   **oxlip** A yellow flower which is a cross between cowslip and primrose. It looks like a large cowslip.

251   **Quite ... woodbine** with lovely honeysuckle arching overhead

252   **musk-roses** wild roses

     eglantine sweet-briar rose

253   **sometime** for some part of

254   **Lulled** gently sent to sleep

255   **throws** throws off, casts, sloughs

     enamelled glossy patterned

256   **Weed** garment

257   **streak** smear

258   **hateful fantasies** unpleasant imaginings

262   **espies** catches sight of

DEMETRIUS   I will not stay thy questions, let me go.   235
            Or, if thou follow me, do not believe
            But I shall do thee mischief in the wood.

                                            [*Exit* DEMETRIUS

HELENA   Ay, in the temple, in the town, the field,
            You do me mischief. Fie Demetrius,
            Your wrongs do set a scandal on my sex.   240
            We cannot fight for love, as men may do;
            We should be wooed, and were not made to woo.
            I'll follow thee, and make a heaven of hell,
            To die upon the hand I love so well.

                                            [*Exit* HELENA

OBERON   Fare thee well nymph. Ere he do leave this grove,   245
            Thou shalt fly him, and he shall seek thy love.

            Enter PUCK

            Hast thou the flower there? Welcome wanderer.

PUCK   Ay, there it is.

OBERON   I pray thee give it me.
            I know a bank whereon the wild thyme blows,
            Where oxlips and the nodding violet grows,   250
            Quite over-canopied with luscious woodbine,
            With sweet musk-roses, and with eglantine.
            There sleeps Titania sometime of the night,
            Lulled in those flowers with dances and delight.
            And there the snake throws her enamelled skin,   255
            Weed wide enough to wrap a fairy in.
            And with the juice of this I'll streak her eyes,
            And make her full of hateful fantasies.
            Take thou some of it, and seek through this grove:
            A sweet Athenian lady is in love   260
            With a disdainful youth. Anoint his eyes,
            But do it when the next thing he espies
            May be the lady. Thou shalt know the man

Puck will know the man Oberon has in mind because he will be wearing Athenian clothes. Puck must carry out his instructions carefully.

265 **Effect it** Carry it out

266 **fond on** in love with, infatuated with

267 **look thou** make sure

Act 2 scene 1

Plot lines

This scene introduces the main characters of the fourth plot line: Oberon, Titania, and Puck. So we can add their story to the plot lines table we started at the end of Act 1:

Plot line 1: **Theseus and Hippolyta**	Plot line 2: **The young lovers**	Plot line 3: **Bottom and his friends**	Plot line 4: **Oberon and Titania**
Theseus has won Hippolyta in battle.	Egeus says that Hermia must marry Demetrius or die.	Quince and the actors meet in the woods to plan their play.	Oberon and Titania are King and Queen of the fairies.

Work with a partner

1 Get the plot lines table you made earlier (or make a new one).

2 On the facing page there is a list of new plot points. As before, they are in the wrong order. Put them in the table in the right order.

By the Athenian garments he hath on.
Effect it with some care, that he may prove   265
More fond on her than she upon her love.
And look thou meet me ere the first cock crow.

PUCK   Fear not my lord, your servant shall do so.

[Exeunt

Plot points

- Oberon sends Puck off with the magic juice to make Demetrius fall madly in love with Helena. 7
- Demetrius and Helena arrive. She is still in love with him and he is trying to escape. 6
- Oberon goes in search of Titania to use the magic juice on her. 4
- Oberon is angry because Titania is keeping a 'changeling' child and will not hand the boy over to him. 3
- Titania says that their quarrelling is the cause of the terrible weather they have been having: all the seasons are topsy-turvy. 2
- Oberon and Titania meet and quarrel. They accuse each other of being unfaithful. 1
- Oberon sends Puck to find a special plant with magic powers. 5

Theme: magic and mystery

This scene introduces us to the magical kingdom of Oberon and Titania. How audiences and readers react to *A Midsummer Night's Dream* depends very much on how they feel about this fairy world. Is it:

this?   or this?

Is it:

1   childish fun, like a pantomime?

2   spooky and threatening, like a horror story?

3   entertaining and exciting like a fantasy film?

On these two pages we begin to explore these ideas.

Job descriptions

In Act 2 scene 1 we meet four characters from the fairy world: a Fairy, Puck (Robin Goodfellow), Oberon, and Titania. From their conversations we learn what their powers are and how they use them. For example, Puck tells us a lot about himself in these lines:

- 42–57
- 175–6

Work in a group of three

1   Read these lines again.

2   What does Puck tell us he can do? Make a list in a table like the one at the top of the next page. It has been started for you.

3   For each item in the list, find a supporting quotation and write it in the right-hand column.

What Puck does	Supporting quotation	Lines
Scares the village girls		
	I am that merry ... night	43
Changes his shape		

4 Now each take one of the other fairy characters (Fairy, Oberon, Titania) and make a similar table for them.

5 Pass the tables round the group. Use them to make a list of the main features of this magical kingdom.

Staging the magic

So what is the best way to present this part of the play to a modern audience?

Work on your own

1 What do you think 'magic' means? Make a list of at least one example of magic from each of these:

- films
- books
- cartoons
- pictures.

Work in a group of three to five

1 Talk about the lists you have made.

2 Imagine you are designing a theatre production of *A Midsummer Night's Dream*. The director has asked you to produce some ideas about what the magic kingdom might look like. Brainstorm your ideas. Make a list of the elements you could include, such as:

- colours and shapes
- scenery
- costume materials
- sounds and music
- special effects.

3 Prepare a presentation explaining your ideas of the scenery and costumes for the magic kingdom.

4 Present your ideas to the rest of the class.

Titania gives her fairies their tasks for the night and then they sing her a lullaby.

1   **a roundel** a dance in a circle

2   **hence** away

3   **cankers** grubs

4   **war with rere-mice** fight with bats

        leathern wings wings like leather

5   **keep back** chase off

6   **clamorous** noisy

        wonders is amazed

7   **quaint** unusual

8   **offices** duties

9   **double tongue** Snakes have a forked tongue.

10   **Thorny** prickly

11   **Newts** Small amphibians which spend some time on land, but go into water to breed.

        blind-worms Slow-worms: not worms, not snakes, not venomous, really legless lizards.

13   **Philomel** In Greek **myth** (see Glossary p. 227) she was changed into a nightingale, after many sufferings.

18   **nigh** near

Scene ❷

The wood

Enter TITANIA, *with her train*

TITANIA Come, now a roundel and a fairy song;
Then, for the third part of a minute, hence –
Some to kill cankers in the musk-rose buds,
Some war with rere-mice for their leathern wings,
To make my small elves coats, and some keep
    back   5
The clamorous owl, that nightly hoots and
    wonders
At our quaint spirits. Sing me now asleep;
Then to your offices, and let me rest.

Fairies sing

FIRST FAIRY
You spotted snakes with double tongue,
Thorny hedgehogs, be not seen,   10
Newts and blind-worms do no wrong –
Come not near our Fairy Queen.
Philomel, with melody,
Sing in our sweet lullaby,
Lulla, lulla, lullaby, lulla, lulla, lullaby;   15
   Never harm,
   Nor spell, nor charm,
Come our lovely lady nigh.
So good night, with lullaby.

When the lullaby is over, one fairy stays on guard and the rest leave. Titania falls asleep and Oberon comes in and squeezes the juice on Titania's eyelids. He hopes she will fall in love with a monster. Oberon leaves and Hermia and Lysander come in. They have lost their way and are exhausted. They plan to sleep until daylight.

20	**Weaving** Spiders spin webs which are incredibly strong.
23	**offence** wrong
26	**stand sentinel** be on guard
29	**Love and languish** fall in love and feel that you are likely to die for his sake
30	**ounce** lynx
	cat civet-cat
31	**Pard** leopard
	boar ... hair wild boar with rough hair and bristly mane
36	**to speak troth** truth to tell
	forgot lost
38	**tarry ... day** wait until it is daylight and more cheerful
39	**Be it ... bed** Yes, that's best – you find somewhere to lie
41	**One ... both** One patch of grass will do for both of us
42	**two bosoms** two hearts
	one troth trusting each other
45	**innocence** goodwill, honesty

SECOND FAIRY
Weaving spiders come not here;   20
　　Hence you long-legged spinners, hence.
Beetles black approach not near,
　　Worm nor snail, do no offence.
Philomel, with melody, &c.

FIRST FAIRY
Hence away, now all is well.   25
One aloof stand sentinel.

　　　　　　　[*Exeunt Fairies*. TITANIA *sleeps*

Enter OBERON, *and squeezes the flower on* TITANIA'S
eyelids

OBERON　　What thou seest when thou dost wake,
Do it for thy true-love take;
Love and languish for his sake.
Be it ounce, or cat, or bear,   30
Pard, or boar with bristled hair,
In thy eye that shall appear
When thou wakest, it is thy dear.
Wake when some vile thing is near.

　　　　　　　　　　　　　　　[*Exit*

Enter LYSANDER *and* HERMIA

LYSANDER　　Fair love, you faint 'with wandering in the wood,   35
And to speak troth I have forgot our way.
We'll rest us Hermia, if you think it good,
And tarry for the comfort of the day.

HERMIA　　Be it so Lysander; Find you out a bed,
For I upon this bank will rest my head.   40

LYSANDER　　One turf shall serve as pillow for us both,
One heart, one bed, two bosoms, and one troth.

HERMIA　　Nay good Lysander, for my sake, my dear,
Lie further off yet, do not lie so near.

LYSANDER　　O take the sense, sweet, of my innocence.   45

Lysander and Hermia lie down some way apart, at her insistence. They fall asleep. Puck comes along, looking for Demetrius. He assumes, as these two lovers are so far apart, that they must be Demetrius and Helena.

46	**Love ... conference** When lovers talk they have the same understanding as each other just because they are in love
47	**knit** joined
49	**Two ... oath** Two hearts linked with one vow
50	**single troth** one faith, one loyalty
51–2	**Then ... lie** So don't prevent me from sleeping next to you, because, lying in that way I'm not telling a lie – **a play on words** (see Glossary p. 228)
53	**riddles very prettily** tells very clever riddles
54	**beshrew** put a curse on
	manners behaviour
55	**If ... lied** I certainly didn't mean to say Lysander was lying
56	**gentle ... courtesy** kind friend, for affection to me and politeness
58	**separation** distance
59	**Becomes** is proper for
	virtuous honourable
60	**So ... distant** sleep over there
61	**Thy love ... end** May your love never change until your dear life ends
63	**end life ... loyalty** let my life end when I stop being loyal to you
64	**sleep give thee** may sleep give you
68	**approve** test
69	**stirring** encouraging
71	**Weeds of Athens** Athenian clothes
75	**dank** damp
76	**durst not lie** doesn't dare to lie
77	**lack-love, this kill-courtesy** this boorish man
78	**Churl** You villain!

Love takes the meaning in love's conference.
I mean that my heart unto yours is knit,
So that but one heart we can make of it.
Two bosoms interchained with an oath;
So then two bosoms, and a single troth.   50
Then by your side no bed-room me deny;
For lying so, Hermia, I do not lie.

HERMIA   Lysander riddles very prettily.
Now much beshrew my manners and my pride,
If Hermia meant to say Lysander lied.   55
But gentle friend, for love and courtesy
Lie further off, in human modesty.
Such separation as may well be said
Becomes a virtuous bachelor and a maid,
So far be distant; and good night sweet friend. 60
Thy love ne'er alter till thy sweet life end.

LYSANDER   Amen, amen, to that fair prayer, say I;
And then end life when I end loyalty.
Here is my bed; sleep give thee all his rest.

HERMIA   With half that wish the wisher's eyes be pressed.   65

[They sleep

Enter PUCK

PUCK   Through the forest have I gone,
But Athenian found I none,
On whose eyes I might approve
This flower's force in stirring love.
Night and silence – Who is here?   70
Weeds of Athens he doth wear.
This is he, my master said,
Despised the Athenian maid.
And here the maiden, sleeping sound,
On the dank and dirty ground.   75
Pretty soul, she durst not lie
Near this lack-love, this kill-courtesy.
Churl, upon thy eyes I throw

Puck treats Lysander with the magic juice and goes to report back to Oberon. Demetrius and Helena come running in. She is still trying to attract him, but he runs off. She comes to the conclusion that she must be ugly and can never compare with Hermia. Suddenly she sees Lysander on the ground and wakes him up. Of course he instantly falls in love with her.

79   **owe** own, possess

80–1   **When ... eyelid** Once you wake up may the passionate love you feel keep you awake

84   **Stay** Stop

        though even if

85   **I charge thee hence** I'm telling you to go away

86   **darkling** in the dark

87   **on thy peril** at your own risk

88   **fond** foolish

89   **The more ... grace** The more I ask, the less response I receive

        grace answer to a prayer

90   **whereso'er** wherever

92   **How ... bright?** How did her eyes get so bright?

95   **beasts ... me** animals that I come across

96   **Therefore ... though** So it's hardly surprising that

97   **Do ... thus** flees from me as if I were a monster

98   **dissembling glass** deceptive, deceitful mirror

99   **sphery eyne** eyes like starlight

104   **Transparent** Bright, beautiful; also something that can be seen through

       Nature shows art Nature demonstrates her magic power

105   **That ... heart** so that through your breast I can see your heart

106–7   **O how ... sword** Oh how suitable that evil name is to die, run through by my sword

[Puts the juice on LYSANDER'S *eyelids*

	All the power this charm doth owe.	
	When thou wakest, let love forbid	80
	Sleep his seat on thy eyelid.	
	So awake when I am gone;	
	For I must now to Oberon.	*[Exit*

Enter DEMETRIUS *and* HELENA, *running*

HELENA	Stay, though thou kill me, sweet Demetrius.	
DEMETRIUS	I charge thee hence, do not haunt me thus.	85
HELENA	O wilt thou darkling leave me? Do not so.	
DEMETRIUS	Stay, on thy peril; I alone will go.	*[Exit*
HELENA	O, I am out of breath in this fond chase.	
	The more my prayer, the lesser is my grace.	
	Happy is Hermia, wheresoe'er she lies;	90
	For she hath blessed and attractive eycs.	
	How came her eyes so bright? Not with salt tears;	
	If so, my eyes are oftener washed than hers.	
	No, no, I am as ugly as a bear,	
	For beasts that meet me run away for fear.	95
	Therefore no marvel though Demetrius	
	Do, as a monster, fly my presence thus.	
	What wicked and dissembling glass of mine	
	Made me compare with Hermia's sphery eyne?	
	But who is here? Lysander, on the ground,	100
	Dead, or asleep? I see no blood, no wound.	
	Lysander, if you live, good sir awake.	
LYSANDER	*[Awaking]* And run through fire I will for thy	
	sweet sake.	
	Transparent Helena, Nature shows art,	
	That through thy bosom makes me see thy heart.	105
	Where is Demetrius? O how fit a word	
	Is that vile name to perish on my sword.	
HELENA	Do not say so, Lysander, say not so.	

Lysander tells Helena he now loves her and not Hermia. Helena thinks he is mocking her, but he insists she is the only one for him. Helena is angry at being so badly treated by both men and goes off. Lysander leaves Hermia sleeping on the ground and follows, saying he now hates Hermia.

109	**What though** What if
114	**raven** A black bird, one of the crow family. Hermia is often referred to as being dark-complexioned and Helena as fair-skinned.
115	**The will ... swayed** We know, and Lysander does not, that magic and not reason has changed his affections. This is a form of **dramatic irony** (see Glossary p. 225).
	will desire
118	**till ... reason** until now I have not matured enough to use my reason
119	**touching ... skill** now that I am reaching the high point of my capabilities
120	**marshal ... will** guide for my desires
121–2	**where I ... book** where I read the tales that love tells, written where love is in its purest form
123	**keen** bitter
128	**flout my insufficiency** jeer at my inadequacy
129	**Good troth ... good sooth** Both mean 'truly', 'indeed'.
132	**gentleness** courteous behaviour
134	**of another** by another man
137	**a surfeit** excess, too much
137–8	**For as ... brings** Just as when we eat too much sweet stuff, the stomach comes to hate the very idea of more
139–40	**as the heresies ... deceive** as the false beliefs that men reject are hated most by those who were once taken in by them
143	**address** direct
	might force

What though he love your Hermia? Lord, what
    though?
Yet Hermia still loves you; then be content.   110

LYSANDER   Content with Hermia? No, I do repent
The tedious minutes I with her have spent.
Not Hermia, but Helena I love.
Who will not change a raven for a dove?
The will of man is by his reason swayed;   115
And reason says you are the worthier maid.
Things growing are not ripe until their season;
So I, being young, till now ripe not to reason;
And touching now the point of human skill,
Reason becomes the marshal to my will,   120
And leads me to your eyes, where I o'erlook
Love's stories, written in love's richest book.

HELENA   Wherefore was I to this keen mockery born?
When at your hands did I deserve this scorn?
Is't not enough, is't not enough, young man,   125
That I did never, no nor never can
Deserve a sweet look from Demetrius' eye,
But you must flout my insufficiency?
Good troth you do me wrong, good sooth you do,
In such disdainful manner me to woo.   130
But fare you well; perforce I must confess
I thought you lord of more true gentleness.
O, that a lady, of one man refused,
Should of another therefore be abused.   [*Exit*

LYSANDER   She sees not Hermia. Hermia, sleep thou there,   135
And never mayst thou come Lysander near.
For, as a surfeit of the sweetest things
The deepest loathing to the stomach brings;
Or as the heresies that men do leave
Are hated most of those they did deceive;   140
So thou, my surfeit and my heresy,
Of all be hated; but the most of me.
And, all my powers address your love and might,

Lysander leaves to follow Helena. Hermia wakes up from a nightmare in which a snake seemed to be eating her heart while Lysander watched, smiling. She calls for Lysander and then realises that he has gone. Still in terror from the dream she goes off to try to find him.

147	**Ay me, for pity!** Oh horror!
148	**quake** tremble
149	**Methought** I thought
150	**cruel prey** as it horribly preyed on me
151	**removed?** gone?
153	**Alack** Alas
	an … hear if you can hear me
154	**swoon** faint
155	**Then … perceive** Now I realise
	nigh nearby

Act 2 scene 2

Plot lines

This scene adds more twists to the complicated plotting of the play. So we can add these to the plot lines table we started at the end of Act 1:

Plot line 1: **Theseus and Hippolyta**	Plot line 2: **The young lovers**	Plot line 3: **Bottom and his friends**	Plot line 4: **Oberon and Titania**
Theseus has won Hippolyta in battle.	Egeus says that Hermia must marry Demetrius or die.	Quince and the actors meet in the woods to plan their play.	Oberon and Titania are King and Queen of the fairies.

To honour Helen and to be her knight.   [*Exit*

HERMIA   [*Awaking*] Help me Lysander, help me; do thy
      best   145
To pluck this crawling serpent from my breast.
Ay me, for pity! What a dream was here!
Lysander look, how I do quake with fear.
Methought a serpent ate my heart away,
And you sat smiling at his cruel prey.   150
Lysander! What, removed? Lysander, lord!
What, out of hearing, gone? No sound, no word?
Alack where are you? Speak, an if you hear.
Speak, of all loves! I swoon almost with fear.
No? Then I well perceive you are not nigh;   155
Either death or you I'll find immediately.

               [*Exit*

Work with a partner

1 Get your plot lines table (or make a new one).
2 Place the plot points below in the right order.

Plot points

- Lysander wakes up and sees Helena. Because of the love juice he falls madly in love with her.
- Puck finds Lysander and Hermia and puts love juice on Lysander's eyes, thinking he is Demetrius.
- Helena is horrified and runs off, followed by Lysander.
- Oberon puts love juice on Titania's eyes.
- Demetrius arrives, still pursued by Helena. But at last he escapes, leaving her behind.
- Titania arrives in another part of the forest and is sung to sleep by her fairies.
- Hermia awakes from a nightmare and finds herself alone.
- Hermia and Lysander arrive and fall asleep.

The love tangle

By the end of this scene the tangle has got worse. So the diagram you drew at the end of Act 1 scene 1 is now out of date. Lower down this page there is:

- a new version of the diagram
- a list of words that should be in the empty boxes.

Work with a partner

1   Copy out the diagram onto a large sheet of paper.

2   Read through Act 2 scene 2 again and work out where the words should go.

3   Write them in the correct boxes.

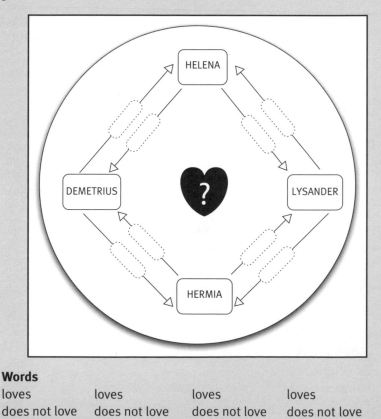

Words

loves	loves	loves	loves
does not love	does not love	does not love	does not love

Plot summary quiz

The 11 quotations below sum up the story of the play so far.

1 Work out the correct order for them.

2 Work out who said each one.

A

Ill met by moonlight, proud Titania.

B

She never had so sweet a changeling. And jealous Oberon would have the child…

C

What thou seest when thou dost wake, Do it for thy true-love take…

D

Help me Lysander, help me; do thy best
To pluck this crawling serpent from my breast.

E

Fetch me that flower; the herb I showed thee once…

F

Full of vexation come I, with complaint Against my child…

G

If thou lovest me then, Steal forth thy father's house tomorrow night…

H

Marry, our play is, 'The most lamentable comedy, and most cruel death of Pyramus and Thisby'.

I

I am sick when I do look on thee.

J

Churl, upon thy eyes I throw All the power this charm doth owe.

K

You have her father's love, Demetrius; Let me have Hermia's. Do you marry him.

Titania is lying asleep, invisible to humans. The workmen come in to start their rehearsal. Bottom is concerned that the ladies of the court will not be able to stand the sight of Pyramus killing himself. They agree to write a reassuring prologue. Then there is the further worry that the ladies will be afraid of the lion.

1	**Are ... met?** Are we all here?
2	**Pat** As arranged, on the dot
	convenient suitable
3	**green plot** patch of grass
4	**hawthorn-brake** hawthorn bush
	tiring-house dressing room; in the Elizabethan theatre it would be directly behind the stage.
7	**bully** my friend
11	**abide** face
12	**By'r lakin** by our Lady
	parlous perilous, dangerous
15	**Not a whit** Not a bit of it
	device scheme
23	**eight and six** lines of eight and six syllables
27	**I promise you** I can tell you

Act Three

Scene 1

The wood

TITANIA *lying asleep*

Enter QUINCE, SNUG, BOTTOM, FLUTE, SNOUT, *and* STARVELING

BOTTOM   Are we all met?

QUINCE   Pat, pat; and here's a marvellous convenient place
             for our rehearsal. This green plot shall be our stage,
             this hawthorn-brake our tiring-house, and we will
             do it in action, as we will do it before the duke.   5

BOTTOM   Peter Quince.

QUINCE   What sayest thou, bully Bottom?

BOTTOM   There are things in this comedy of Pyramus and
             Thisby that will never please. First, Pyramus
             must draw a sword to kill himself; which the   10
             ladies cannot abide. How answer you that?

SNOUT   By'r lakin, a parlous fear.

STARVELING   I believe we must leave the killing out, when all is
             done.

BOTTOM   Not a whit, I have a device to make all well.   15
             Write me a prologue, and let the prologue seem
             to say, we will do no harm with our swords, and
             that Pyramus is not killed indeed. And for the
             more better assurance, tell them that I Pyramus
             am not Pyramus, but Bottom the weaver; this   20
             will put them out of fear.

QUINCE   Well, we will have such a prologue, and it shall
             be written in eight and six.

BOTTOM   No, make it two more; let it be written in eight
             and eight.   25

SNOUT   Will not the ladies be afeard of the lion?

STARVELING   I fear it, I promise you.

They decide to explain that the lion is really Snug the joiner. The next problem is how to show it is moonlight indoors. They decide one of them must act the moon. They need a wall as well.

29   **God shield us** Heaven preserve us

31   **wild-fowl** creature

32   **look to 't** attend to it

37   **defect** Bottom means 'effect'.

39   **my life for yours** I'd bet my life on it

40   **hither** here

      it were ... life my life would be at risk

45   **to bring ... chamber** to get moonlight to shine into the room; Quince has a serious point because at The Globe plays were performed in daylight. They would have the similar problem in the great hall of the palace.

48   **almanac** calendar

51   **casement** part of the large window that can be opened, a window-light

51–2 **great chamber** state room

54–5 **bush of thorns** Traditionally carried by the man in the moon.

55   **lanthorn** lantern (often made of horn, through which a candle could show its light)

56   **disfigure** He means figure (represent).

60   **chink** crack, hole

BOTTOM	Masters, you ought to consider with yourselves – to bring in, God shield us, a lion among ladies, is a most dreadful thing. For there is not a more fearful wild-fowl than your lion living; and we ought to look to 't.
SNOUT	Therefore another prologue must tell he is not a lion.
BOTTOM	Nay, you must name his name, and half his face must be seen through the lion's neck, and he himself must speak through, saying thus, or to the same defect 'Ladies,' or 'Fair ladies, I would wish you,' or, 'I would request you,' or, 'I would entreat you, not to fear, not to tremble; my life for yours. If you think I come hither as a lion, it were pity of my life. No, I am no such thing, I am a man as other men are;' and there indeed let him name his name, and tell them plainly he is Snug the joiner.
QUINCE	Well, it shall be so. But there is two hard things; that is, to bring the moonlight into a chamber; for, you know, Pyramus and Thisby meet by moonlight.
SNOUT	Doth the moon shine that night we play our play?
BOTTOM	A calendar, a calendar, look in the almanac; find out moonshine, find out moonshine.
QUINCE	Yes, it doth shine that night.
BOTTOM	Why then may you leave a casement of the great chamber window, where we play, open, and the moon may shine in at the casement.
QUINCE	Ay, or else one must come in with a bush of thorns and a lanthorn, and say he comes to disfigure, or to present, the person of moonshine. Then, there is another thing we must have a wall in the great chamber, for Pyramus and Thisby, says the story, did talk through the chink of a wall.
SNOUT	You can never bring in a wall. What say you, Bottom?

30

35

40

45

50

55

60

They decide one of them must be the wall. They get ready to rehearse. Puck, who is invisible to humans, comes in and decides to watch. He says he will take part if he feels like it. Quince starts to run his rehearsal.

64–5 **plaster ... loam ... rough-cast** All three are substances used on exterior walls, and made chiefly of clay, sand and straw mixed to a paste with water.

66 **cranny** crack, slit

71 **brake** bush i.e. the hawthorn bush which is their dressing-room

73 **hempen home-spuns** country bumpkins (Hemp when spun and woven produced a rough cloth.)

75 **toward** in preparation

auditor listener

78 **odious savours sweet** Bottom has got the wrong word again. 'Odious' means 'unpleasant' whereas all three words – 'odours', 'savours' and 'sweet' – imply scented, sweet-smelling, perfumed.

82 **by and by** in a moment, shortly

83 **e'er** ever

85 **marry** indeed, to be sure

90 **brisky juvenal** lively youth

eke also

Jew It seems to be just a handy ending to rhyme with 'hue'.

92 **Ninny** fool; Pyramus and Thisby are to meet at Ninus' tomb. He was the mythical founder of the city of Nineveh.

BOTTOM Some man or other must present wall; and let him have some plaster, or some loam, or some rough-cast about him, to signify wall; or let him hold his fingers thus, and through that cranny shall Pyramus and Thisby whisper.

QUINCE If that may be, then all is well. Come, sit down, every mother's son, and rehearse your parts. Pyramus, you begin. When you have spoken your speech, enter into that brake; and so every one according to his cue.

Enter PUCK

PUCK What hempen home-spuns have we swaggering
here,
So near the cradle of the Fairy Queen?
What, a play toward! I'll be an auditor,
An actor too perhaps, if I see cause.

QUINCE Speak, Pyramus, Thisby stand forth.

BOTTOM Thisby, the flowers of odious savours sweet –

QUINCE Odours, odours.

BOTTOM Odours savours sweet,
So hath thy breath, my dearest Thisby dear.
But hark, a voice; stay thou but here awhile,
And by and by I will to thee appear. [*Exit*

PUCK A stranger Pyramus than e'er played here. [*Exit*

FLUTE Must I speak now?

QUINCE Ay marry, must you. For you must understand he goes but to see a noise that he heard, and is to come again.

FLUTE Most radiant Pyramus, most lily-white of hue,
Of colour like the red rose on triumphant briar,
Most brisky juvenal, and eke most lovely Jew,
As true as truest horse, that yet would never tire,
I'll meet thee, Pyramus, at Ninny's tomb.

QUINCE 'Ninus' tomb', man. Why you must not speak

Bottom, in his role as the lover, Pyramus, is waiting for his next cue. When he enters, Puck has used his magic on him and he has an ass's head. His friends are terrified and rush off. Puck intends to enjoy himself by leading them on a nightmarish journey. Bottom is bewildered at his friends' reaction, but decides to sing so they can see he is not afraid.

98   **fair** handsome

101   **about a round** a dance round and about

103   **briar** thorns

107   **knavery** silly trick

112   **translated** transformed

118   **ousel cock** male blackbird

	that yet; that you answer to Pyramus. You speak	
	all your part at once, cues and all. Pyramus	95
	enter, your cue is past; it is 'never tire.'	

FLUTE   O – as true as truest horse, that yet would never tire.

Enter PUCK, *and* BOTTOM *with an ass's head*

BOTTOM If I were fair, Thisby, I were only thine.

QUINCE O monstrous! O strange! We are haunted. Pray,
        masters fly, masters! Help!   100

[*Exeunt* QUINCE, SNUG, FLUTE, SNOUT, *and* STARVELING

PUCK   I'll follow you, I'll lead you about a round,
          Through bog, through bush, through brake,
            through briar.
        Sometime a horse I'll be, sometime a hound,
          A hog, a headless bear, sometime a fire.
        And neigh, and bark, and grunt, and roar, and   105
          burn,
        Like horse, hound, hog, bear, fire at every turn.
                                                   [*Exit

BOTTOM Why do they run away? This is a knavery of them
        to make me afeard.

Enter SNOUT

SNOUT   O Bottom, thou art changed. What do I see on thee?

BOTTOM What do you see? You see an ass-head of your   110
        own, do you?   [*Exit* SNOUT

Enter QUINCE

QUINCE Bless thee Bottom, bless thee. Thou art translated.
                                                   [*Exit

BOTTOM I see their knavery. This is to make an ass of me,
        to fright me, if they could. But I will not stir from
        this place, do what they can. I will walk up and   115
        down here, and I will sing, that they shall hear I
        am not afraid.   [*Sings
          The ousel cock so black of hue,

Bottom's song wakes up Titania, who immediately falls in love with him. Bottom sings to her and then says he wants to get out of the wood. She wants him to stay and can force him to do so. She promises him servants from among her fairies.

119   **orange-tawny bill** yellowish-brown beak (Orange-tawny is the colour of one of the beards Bottom was suggesting he could use in the play.)

120   **throstle** thrush

121   **little quill** small piping voice

124   **plain-song cuckoo** the cuckoo which sings a simple tune; the sound of the cuckoo was by tradition supposed to sound like 'cuckold' and to be telling husbands that their wives were deceiving them. This song suggests there are many men who cannot deny that this has happened.

126   **dares ... nay** cannot deny it

127   **set his wit** use his intelligence

128   **give ... lie** accuse the bird of lying

131   **enamoured of** attracted by

132   **enthralled to** captivated by, delighted by

133   **thy ... force** the power of your good qualities

         perforce ... me forces me

139   **gleek** jest, make a joke

143   **to serve ... turn** for my needs

147   **tend upon** wait on, serve

         state rank

150   **the deep** the ocean

152   **purge ... grossness** get rid of your human clumsiness

            With orange-tawny bill,
            The throstle with his note so true,   120
                The wren with little quill –

TITANIA   [*Awaking*] What angel wakes me from my
            flowery bed?

BOTTOM   [*Sings*]

            The finch, the sparrow, and the lark,
            The plain-song cuckoo grey,
                Whose note full many a man doth mark,   125
                And dares not answer, nay –
        for indeed, who would set his wit to so foolish a
        bird? Who would give a bird the lie, though he
        cry 'cuckoo' never so?

TITANIA   I pray thee, gentle mortal, sing again.   130
        Mine ear is much enamoured of thy note;
        So is mine eye enthralled to thy shape,
        And thy fair virtue's force perforce doth move me,
        On the first view to say, to swear, I love thee.

BOTTOM   Methinks mistress, you should have little reason   135
        for that. And yet, to say the truth, reason and
        love keep little company together now-a-days.
        The more the pity that some honest neighbours
        will not make them friends. Nay, I can gleek
        upon occasion.   140

TITANIA   Thou art as wise as thou art beautiful.

BOTTOM   Not so neither. But if I had wit enough to get out of
        this wood, I have enough to serve mine own turn.

TITANIA   Out of this wood do not desire to go.
        Thou shalt remain here, whether thou wilt or no.   145
        I am a spirit of no common rate.
        The summer still doth tend upon my state,
        And I do love thee; therefore, go with me.
        I'll give thee fairies to attend on thee;
        And they shall fetch thee jewels from the deep,   150
        And sing, while thou on pressed flowers dost sleep.
        And I will purge thy mortal grossness so,

Titania calls on four fairies to wait on Bottom. He finds something pleasant to say to each of them.

153   **thou ... spirit go** you will move like a creature of the air

157   **Hop ... eyes** when he walks about, leap and play about in his sight

158   **dewberries** Berries a bit like blackberries; they can still be found in the countryside. The fruits are smaller but plumper than blackberries and have a whitish bloom on the skin.

160   **humble-bees** Bumble-bees with honey-bags containing nectar.

161   **for night-tapers ... thighs** collect beeswax for candles

166   **Nod** Bow your head

       courtesies kindnesses

168   **I cry ... heartily** I thank you most gratefully

168–9   **I beseech ... name** I beg to know your worship's name (Bottom, totally confused, is making up 'polite' conversation as well as he can.)

171   **I shall ... acquaintance** I shall hope to see more of you

172   **If I ... finger** It is possible to reduce the flow of blood in a small cut by using a cobweb.

175   **Squash** unripe pea pod

176   **Peascod** ripe pea pod

177   **Peaseblossom** the flower of the pea plant

177–8   **I shall ... too** I shall hope to see more of you too

That thou shalt like an airy spirit go.
Peaseblossom, Cobweb, Moth, and Mustardseed!

Enter PEASEBLOSSOM, COBWEB, MOTH, *and* MUSTARDSEED

PEASEBLOSSOM   Ready

COBWEB   And I.

MOTH   And I.

MUSTARDSEED   And I.

ALL   Where shall we go?   155

TITANIA   Be kind and courteous to this gentleman,
Hop in his walks and gambol in his eyes,
Feed him with apricots and dewberries,
With purple grapes, green figs, and mulberries.
The honey-bags steal from the humble-bees,   160
And for night-tapers crop their waxen thighs,
And light them at the fiery glow-worms' eyes,
To have my love to bed and to arise;
And pluck the wings from painted butterflies,
To fan the moonbeams from his sleeping eyes.   165
Nod to him elves, and do him courtesies.

PEASEBLOSSOM   Hail, mortal!

COBWEB   Hail!

MOTH   Hail!

MUSTARDSEED   Hail!

BOTTOM   I cry your worships mercy heartily. I beseech
your worship's name.

COBWEB   Cobweb.   170

BOTTOM   I shall desire you of more acquaintance, good
Master Cobweb. If I cut my finger, I shall make
bold with you. Your name honest gentleman?

PEASEBLOSSOM   Peaseblossom.

BOTTOM   I pray you commend me to Mistress Squash   175
your mother, and to Master Peascod your father.
Good Master Peaseblossom, I shall desire you of

When Bottom has finished greeting all the fairies Titania tells them to lead him away in silence.

180   **Mustardseed** The seed of the mustard plant, ground to make mustard with water added.

182   **patience** suffering

182–4   **That same ... house** Oxen have eaten many of your family (Mustard is a plant with yellow flowers, growing in the fields.)

184–5   **your kindred ... now** Your sort have made my eyes water before now (either from eating strong mustard, or from its use as a poultice on inflamed skin)

187   **bower** a shady arbour (the bank where Titania rests)

188   **The moon ... eye** It looks as though the moon is about to drop dew

190   **Lamenting ... chastity** weeping because 1) they have been abused, or 2) they have been forced to remain chaste

191   **Tie ... tongue** Make sure my love is silenced

more acquaintance too. Your name I beseech you, sir?

MUSTARDSEED   Mustardseed.   180

BOTTOM   Good Master Mustardseed, I know your patience well. That same cowardly, giant-like ox-beef hath devoured many a gentleman of your house. I promise you your kindred hath made my eyes water ere now. I desire you of   185 more acquaintance, good Master Mustardseed.

TITANIA   Come wait upon, lead him to my bower.
The moon methinks looks with a watery eye,
And when she weeps, weeps every little flower,
Lamenting some enforced chastity.   190
Tie up my love's tongue, bring him silently.

[Exeunt

Act 3 scene 1

Plot lines

In this scene, two of the plot lines come together. So we can add these to the plot lines table we started at the end of Act 1:

Plot line 1: **Theseus and Hippolyta**	Plot line 2: **The young lovers**	Plot line 3: **Bottom and his friends**	Plot line 4: **Oberon and Titania**
Theseus has won Hippolyta in battle.	Egeus says that Hermia must marry Demetrius or die.	Quince and the actors meet in the woods to plan their play.	Oberon and Titania are King and Queen of the fairies.

Work with a partner

1 Get your plot lines table (or make a new one).

2 Below there is a list of new plot points. As before, they are in the wrong order. Put them in the table in the right order.

Plot points

- Puck watches the rehearsal. He plots some mischief.

- Titania leads Bottom off to her bower.

- Bottom is completely confused at first, but is delighted to meet Titania's fairy followers.

- The workmen actors meet to rehearse.

- When it is Bottom's turn to enter, he appears with an ass's head instead of his own.

- Left alone, Bottom sings himself a song.

- Titania wakes up and the first person she sees is Bottom. She instantly fall in love with him.

- All the other actors are terrified and run away, but Bottom thinks they are just fooling around.

'This is to make an ass of me'

One of the things people always remember after seeing *A Midsummer Night's Dream* is the scene where Titania falls in love with a creature with a donkey's head. What we get out of a production of the play depends very much on how this is presented on stage. It can be:

- funny, like a pantomime
- grotesque
- rather scary
- a mixture of all three.

Work with a partner

1   You have been commissioned to design the head that Bottom will wear in a new production. The first thing to do is to remind yourselves of what Oberon had planned when he put the love juice on Titania's eyes. You will find Oberon's ideas here:

- Act 2 scene 1 lines 179–82 (page 67)
- Act 2 scene 1 lines 257–8 (page 71)
- Act 2 scene 2 lines 27–34 (page 79)

Read these sections of the script and make a list of adjectives describing the kind of creature Oberon wanted Titania to fall in love with. You can think of your own words and/or choose from this list:

evil	gross	hideous	grotesque
stupid	comic	hateful	weird
fantastic	ugly	horrendous	frightening

2   Think about your list and decide what you want Bottom to look like when Titania falls in love with him. Either make a drawing or write a set of detailed notes describing your design. Write out the quotations from the play that have guided your thoughts alongside your drawing, or in your notes.

When Oberon and Puck meet up, Puck tells him that Titania is in love with a monster. He starts to describe the workmen's rehearsal, and how he fixed an ass's head on Bottom.

2   **what ... eye** what was the next thing she saw

3   **Which ... extremity** which she has to love passionately

5   **What night-rule now** What is going on now it's night

7   **close and consecrated** secret and holy

9   **patches** clowns, fools

       rude mechanicals rough workmen

10   **That ... bread** who have to earn their living

12   **Intended ... day** meant to be performed on Theseus' wedding-day

13   **The shallowest ... sort** The most naive numbskull of that empty-headed bunch

14   **Pyramus ... sport** took the part of Pyramus in their performance

15   **Forsook** left

       brake bush

16–17 **When I ... head** at which point I found a good opportunity to fix an ass's head on his

18   **Anon ... answered** Soon he must respond to Thisby's cue

19   **mimic** actor

19–24 **When they ... fly** When they catch sight of him, his companions rush off. It is just like wild geese noticing the hidden wildfowler; or like a large flock of grey-headed jackdaws which will take off, separate out, cawing at the sound of the gun. This is a vivid **extended image** (see Glossary p. 225).

Scene ❷

The wood

Enter OBERON

OBERON   I wonder if Titania be awaked;
          Then, what it was the next came in her eye,
          Which she must dote on in extremity.

Enter PUCK

          Here comes my messenger. How now, mad
              spirit?
          What night-rule now about this haunted grove?   5

PUCK   My mistress with a monster is in love.
          Near to her close and consecrated bower,
          While she was in her dull and sleeping hour,
          A crew of patches, rude mechanicals,
          That work for bread upon Athenian stalls,   10
          Were met together to rehearse a play
          Intended for great Theseus' nuptial day.
          The shallowest thick-skin of that barren sort,
          Who Pyramus presented, in their sport
          Forsook his scene and entered in a brake,   15
          When I did him at this advantage take.
          An ass's nole I fixed on his head.
          Anon his Thisby must be answered,
          And forth my mimic comes. When they him
              spy,
          As wild geese that the creeping fowler eye,   20

Puck left Bottom in a place where Titania would wake up and fall in love with him. Oberon is delighted. Puck also claims he has dealt with Demetrius, but when Hermia and Demetrius appear, arguing, Oberon realises Puck has made a mistake.

25	**at our stamp** Puck stamped his foot to make his presence heard.
27	**Their sense ... strong** They were so terrified that they almost lost their wits
28	**Made ... wrong** made inanimate objects start to harm them
29	**apparel** clothes
30	**yielders** those who have already given up
31	**distracted fear** bewildered terror
32	**sweet** dear
	translated transformed
33	**so it ... pass** as it happened
34	**straightway loved** immediately fell in love with
35	**could devise** could have planned
36	**latched** anointed, smeared
37	**as I ... do** as I instructed you
38	**I ... sleeping** I did it while he was asleep
40	**she ... eyed** his glance must fall on her
43	**rebuke** scold, reprove
44	**Lay ... foe** Call your bitterest enemy such unkind names
45	**Now ... chide** At present I am only scolding
	use thee treat you
48	**o'er shoes** ankle-deep; Hermia says that if he has started by killing Lysander, he should now wallow in blood and kill her too.

Or russet-pated choughs, many in sort,
Rising and cawing at the gun's report,
Sever themselves, and madly sweep the sky,
So, at his sight, away his fellows fly;
And, at our stamp, here o'er and o'er one falls; 25
He 'murder' cries and help from Athens calls.
Their sense thus weak, lost with their fears thus
    strong,
Made senseless things begin to do them wrong.
For briars and thorns at their apparel snatch,
Some sleeves, some hats; from yielders all things
    catch. 30
I led them on in this distracted fear,
And left sweet Pyramus translated there.
When in that moment, so it came to pass,
Titania waked and straightway loved an ass.

OBERON   This falls out better than I could devise. 35
And but hast thou yet latched the Athenian's eyes
With the love-juice, as I did bid thee do?

PUCK   I took him sleeping – that is finished too –
And the Athenian woman by his side;
That when he waked, of force she must be eyed. 40

Enter HERMIA *and* DEMETRIUS

OBERON   Stand close, this is the same Athenian.

PUCK   This is the woman, but not this the man.

DEMETRIUS   O why rebuke you him that loves you so?
Lay breath so bitter on your bitter foe.

HERMIA   Now I but chide, but I should use thee worse, 45
For thou, I fear, hast given me cause to curse.
If thou hast slain Lysander in his sleep,
Being o'er shoes in blood, plunge in the deep,

Hermia thinks that Demetrius must have killed Lysander. If he was still alive he would never have abandoned her. She goes on accusing Demetrius until he denies it.

50	**true unto** loyal to
51	**stolen** crept silently
52	**as soon** as readily
53–5	**This whole … Antipodes** Hermia's idea is that the moon, creeping through a hole bored right through the centre of the earth, will bring night to what would otherwise be daylight (the moon's brother is the sun) on the other side of the world.
53	**whole** solid
55	**Antipodes** Now Australia and New Zealand.
56	**It cannot be but** It must mean that
57	**dead** deadly
61	**Venus** A planet seen in the sky after sunset as 'the evening star'.
	glimmering shimmering, glittering
67	**Henceforth … men** If Demetrius has killed Lysander he has given up the right to be counted as a human being.
69	**Durst thou have** Would you have dared
70	**O brave touch** A fine stroke
71	**worm** snake
72	**doubler** An adder has a forked (double) tongue, but 'doubler' also means 'more deceitful'.
73	**stung** Adders bite to inject venom into their prey. They do not sting.
74	**passion** passionate outburst
	misprised mood anger which is mistaken
76	**for aught that** as far as
78	**An if … therefore?** Supposing I could, what would I get in return?

	And kill me too.	
	The sun was not so true unto the day	50
	As he to me. Would he have stolen away	
	From sleeping Hermia? I'll believe as soon	
	This whole earth may be bored, and that the moon	
	May through the centre creep, and so displease	
	Her brother's noontide with th' Antipodes.	55
	It cannot be but thou hast murdered him.	
	So should a murderer look; so dead, so grim.	
DEMETRIUS	So should the murdered look, and so should I,	
	Pierced through the heart with your stern cruelty.	
	Yet you, the murderer, look as bright, as clear,	60
	As yonder Venus in her glimmering sphere.	
HERMIA	What's this to my Lysander? Where is he?	
	Ah good Demetrius, wilt thou give him me?	
DEMETRIUS	I had rather give his carcass to my hounds.	
HERMIA	Out dog, out cur! Thou drivest me past the bounds	65
	Of maiden's patience. Hast thou slain him then?	
	Henceforth be never numbered among men.	
	O, once tell true; tell true, even for my sake.	
	Durst thou have looked upon him being awake?	
	And hast thou killed him sleeping? O brave touch.	70
	Could not a worm, an adder, do so much?	
	An adder did it; for with doubler tongue	
	Than thine, thou serpent, never adder stung.	
DEMETRIUS	You spend your passion on a misprised mood.	
	I am not guilty of Lysander's blood;	75
	Nor is he dead, for aught that I can tell.	
HERMIA	I pray thee, tell me then that he is well.	
DEMETRIUS	And if I could, what should I get therefore?	
HERMIA	A privilege never to see me more.	
	And from thy hated presence part I so.	80
	See me no more, whether he be dead or no.	

[*Exit*

Demetrius realises there's no point in following her when she is so angry. As he is sad and tired he lies down to sleep. Oberon scolds Puck for treating the wrong man with the juice and sends him to fetch Helena. Meanwhile he treats Demetrius' eyes. Puck returns, saying that he has found Helena and brought her back. Lysander is following her, begging for her love.

82	**no following her** no point in following her
	vein mood
84–7	**So sorrow's ... stay** I am growing more and more sad, heavy-hearted and sleepy, because sorrow has made me miss my sleep. If I accept this offer of sleepiness and stay here it will be some repayment for all the sleep I have lost tonight. 'Heavy' is used here to mean both 'heavy-hearted' and 'sleepy' – **a play on words** (see Glossary p. 228).
87	**tender** offer
88	**quite** completely
90	**misprision** misunderstanding, mistake
	perforce inevitably
	ensue result
92–3	**Then fate ... on oath** Fate directs that for every one man who remains true in love, a million more do not, swearing oaths and breaking them again and again.
96	**fancy-sick** love-sick
	cheer face, complexion
97	**sighs ... dear** It was believed that each sigh caused the loss of a drop of blood.
99	**against** ready for when
101	**Tartar** Central Asian tribe famous for their fierceness in battle.
104	**apple** pupil (of the eye)
105	**espy** catch sight of
107	**Venus** the evening star
109	**remedy** your cure

DEMETRIUS   There is no following her in this fierce vein.
Here therefore for a while I will remain.
So sorrow's heaviness doth heavier grow
For debt that bankrupt sleep doth sorrow owe;   85
Which now in some slight measure it will pay,
It for his tender here I make some stay.

[Lies down and sleeps

OBERON   What hast thou done? Thou hast mistaken quite,
And laid the love-juice on some true-love's sight.
Of thy misprision must perforce ensue   90
Some true love turned, and not a false turned true.

PUCK   Then fate o'er-rules, that one man holding troth,
A million fail, confounding oath on oath.

OBERON   About the wood go swifter than the wind,
And Helena of Athens look thou find.   95
All fancy-sick she is and pale of cheer,
With sighs of love, that costs the fresh blood dear:
By some illusion see thou bring her here.
I'll charm his eyes against she do appear.

PUCK   I go, I go, look how I go,   100
Swifter than arrow from the Tartar's bow.

[Exit

OBERON   Flower of this purple dye,
Hit with Cupid's archery,
Sink in apple of his eye.

[He squeezes the flower on Demetrius' eyes

When his love he doth espy,   105
Let her shine as gloriously
As the Venus of the sky.
When thou wakest, if she be by,
Beg of her for remedy.

Enter PUCK

PUCK   Captain of our fairy band,   110
Helena is here at hand,

Oberon thinks the noise Helena and Lysander are making will wake Demetrius. Puck is looking forward to seeing two men wooing one woman. Helena is protesting that Lysander is only mocking her, when Demetrius wakes up. He too swears love to Helena, praising her beauty.

113	**fee** payment
114	**fond pageant** foolish spectacle
119	**sport alone** unique amusement
121	**preposterously** in the most unlikely way
122	**Why ... scorn?** What makes you think that I am mocking you, when I say I love you?
124–5	**Look ... appears** Whenever I make these vows to you I weep, and those vows which are born out of weeping are born in truth
127	**badge of faith** (the tears already referred to) the symbol of my true love
128	**do ... cunning** are increasing your deceitfulness
129	**When truth kills truth** The new 'truth' contradicts the former 'truth' of his love for Hermia. The conflict is 'devilish-holy' because it contains the holiness of truth and the devilish element that both 'truths' cannot possibly be true.
	fray conflict, battle
131	**you ... weigh** no weight will register (because the scales will be evenly balanced)
133	**tales** stories, falsehoods
135	**give her o'er** abandon her
137	**nymph** beauty
141	**congealed** frozen; light skin was desirable, darker skin was not.
	Taurus A mountain range in Turkey.
142	**turns ... crow** appears black as a crow

	And the youth, mistook by me,	
	Pleading for a lover's fee.	
	Shall we their fond pageant see?	
	Lord, what fools these mortals be!	115
OBERON	Stand aside. The noise they make	
	Will cause Demetrius to awake.	
PUCK	Then will two at once woo one,	
	That must needs be sport alone.	
	And those things do best please me	120
	That befall preposterously.	

Enter LYSANDER *and* HELENA

LYSANDER	Why should you think that I should woo in scorn?	
	Scorn and derision never come in tears.	
	Look when I vow, I weep; and vows so born,	
	In their nativity all truth appears.	125
	How can these things in me seem scorn to you,	
	Bearing the badge of faith to prove them true?	
HELENA	You do advance your cunning more and more.	
	When truth kills truth, O devilish-holy fray!	
	These vows are Hermia's. Will you give her o'er?	130
	Weigh oath with oath, and you will nothing weigh.	
	Your vows to her and me, put in two scales,	
	Will even weigh, and both as light as tales.	
LYSANDER	I had no judgement when to her I swore.	
HELENA	Nor none, in my mind, now you give her o'er.	135
LYSANDER	Demetrius loves her, and he loves not you.	
DEMETRIUS	[*Awaking*] O Helen, goddess, nymph, perfect, divine!	
	To what, my love, shall I compare thine eyne?	
	Crystal is muddy. O how ripe in show	
	Thy lips, those kissing cherries, tempting grow!	140
	That pure congealed white, high Taurus' snow,	
	Fanned with the eastern wind, turns to a crow	
	When thou hold'st up thy hand. O let me kiss	

Helena is angry at her treatment and turns on them both. They both swear they love only her and Hermia counts for nothing. Hermia comes in looking for Lysander.

144	**seal of bliss** confirmation of delight
145	**bent** determined
147	**civil** kind, decent
150	**join in souls** team up
153	**parts** qualities
157	**trim** fine
159	**sort** rank
160	**extort** abuse
161	**you sport** fun, amusement for yourselves
169	**I will none** I don't want anything to do with her
171	**but ... sojourned** merely visited her as a guest
175	**aby it dear** pay dearly for it
177–8	**Dark ... makes** The darkness of night, which robs the eye of its power to see, makes the ear more sensitive

	This princess of pure white, this seal of bliss!	
HELENA	O spite! O hell! I see you all are bent	145
	To set against me for your merriment.	
	If you were civil and knew courtesy,	
	You would not do me thus much injury.	
	Can you not hate me, as I know you do,	
	But you must join in souls to mock me too?	150
	If you were men, as men you are in show,	
	You would not use a gentle lady so;	
	To vow, and swear, and superpraise my parts,	
	When I am sure you hate me with your hearts.	
	You both are rivals, and love Hermia;	155
	And now both rivals, to mock Helena.	
	A trim exploit, a manly enterprise,	
	To conjure tears up in a poor maid's eyes	
	With your derision. None of noble sort	
	Would so offend a virgin, and extort	160
	A poor soul's patience, all to make you sport.	
LYSANDER	You are unkind, Demetrius; be not so,	
	For you love Hermia; this you know I know.	
	And here, with all good will, with all my heart,	
	In Hermia's love I yield you up my part;	165
	And yours of Helena to me bequeath,	
	Whom I do love, and will do till my death.	
HELENA	Never did mockers waste more idle breath.	
DEMETRIUS	Lysander, keep thy Hermia; I will none.	
	If e'er I loved her, all that love is gone.	170
	My heart to her but as guest-wise sojourned,	
	And now to Helen is it home returned,	
	There to remain.	
LYSANDER	Helen, it is not so.	
DEMETRIUS	Disparage not the faith thou dost not know,	
	Lest to thy peril thou aby it dear.	175
	Look where thy love comes; yonder is thy dear.	

Enter HERMIA

| HERMIA | Dark night, that from the eye his function takes, | |

Hermia now learns that Lysander hates her. Her amazement makes Helena think that all three of them have teamed up to make fun of her. She appeals to Hermia to remember what close friends they used to be.

179–80   **Wherein … recompense** Although it causes our sight to fail, it makes our hearing twice as sharp to compensate for this

186   **bide** stay

187   **engilds** makes shine

188   **yon fiery … light** stars; an 'o' was both an orb and a silver spangle.

192   **confederacy** conspiracy, plot

193   **conjoined** joined together, united

194   **fashion** create, make

       sport entertainment

       in spite of me to spite me, to annoy me

197   **bait** tease, torment

       derision mockery

198   **counsel** confidences

200–1   **chid … parting us** scolded time for passing so quickly that it was time to part

203   **artificial** skilful at making things, creative

205   **sampler** a piece of embroidery

208   **incorporate** belonging to one body

210   **union in partition** single person in two bodies

The ear more quick of apprehension makes.
Wherein it doth impair the seeing sense,
It pays the hearing double recompense. 180
Thou art not by mine eye, Lysander, found;
Mine ear, I thank it, brought me to thy sound.
But why unkindly didst thou leave me so?

LYSANDER Why should he stay whom love doth press to go?

HERMIA What love could press Lysander from my side? 185

LYSANDER Lysander's love, that would not let him bide,
Fair Helena, who more engilds the night
Than all yon fiery oes and eyes of light.
Why seek'st thou me? Could not this make thee
    know,
The hate I bare thee made me leave thee so? 190

HERMIA You speak not as you think; it cannot be.

HELENA Lo, she is one of this confederacy.
Now I perceive they have conjoined all three
To fashion this false sport in spite of me.
Injurious Hermia, most ungrateful maid, 195
Have you conspired, have you with these contrived
To bait me with this foul derision?
Is all the counsel that we two have shared,
The sisters' vows, the hours that we have spent,
When we have chid the hasty-footed time 200
For parting us – O, is all forgot?
All school-days' friendship, childhood innocence?
We, Hermia, like two artificial gods,
Have with our needles created both one flower,
Both on one sampler, sitting on one cushion, 205
Both warbling of one song, both in one key,
As if our hands, our sides, voices, and minds
Had been incorporate. So we grew together,
Like to a double cherry, seeming parted,
But yet an union in partition, 210
Two lovely berries moulded on one stem.
So with two seeming bodies, but one heart,

Hermia is completely at a loss to understand what is happening. Helena thinks it's all a cruel plot to have a good joke at her expense. She decides to leave. Lysander begs her to stay.

213–14   **Two ... crest** An image from heraldry. 'The first' refers back to 'bodies'. A shield, used as a coat of arms, may have two or four divisions – halves or quarters – and while the same device may appear twice, the whole design appears under one crest and belongs to one person.

215   **rent ... asunder** tear our friendship apart

218   **chide** scold

225   **even but now** just now, a moment ago

        spurn ... foot kick me aside

230   **forsooth** indeed

231   **But ... setting on** except through your encouragement

232   **grace** favour

233   **hung upon** loaded down with

234   **miserable most** the most miserable of women

237   **persever** carry on

        counterfeit put on falsely

238   **Make ... me** Pull faces at me

239   **hold ... jest up** carry on with your charming little joke

240   **chronicled** written about

242   **argument** object of cruel joking

244   **remedy** put right

Two of the first, like coats in heraldry,
Due but to one, and crowned with one crest.
And will you rent our ancient love asunder,   215
To join with men in scorning your poor friend?
It is not friendly, 'tis not maidenly.
Our sex, as well as I, may chide you for it,
Though I alone do feel the injury.

HERMIA   I am amazed at your passionate words.   220
I scorn you not. It seems that you scorn me.

HELENA   Have you not set Lysander, as in scorn,
To follow me, and praise my eyes and face?
And made your other love, Demetrius,
Who even but now did spurn me with his foot,   225
To call me goddess, nymph, divine, and rare,
Precious, celestial? Wherefore speaks he this
To her he hates? And wherefore doth Lysander
Deny your love, so rich within his soul,
And tender me, forsooth, affection,   230
But by your setting on, by your consent?
What though I be not so in grace as you,
So hung upon with love, so fortunate,
But miserable most, to love unloved?
This you should pity rather than despise.   235

HERMIA   I understand not what you mean by this.

HELENA   Ay, do, persever, counterfeit sad looks.
Make mouths upon me when I turn my back.
Wink each at other, hold the sweet jest up.
This sport well carried, shall be chronicled.   240
If you have any pity, grace, or manners,
You would not make me such an argument.
But fare ye well, 'tis partly mine own fault,
Which death or absence soon shall remedy.

LYSANDER   Stay gentle Helena, hear my excuse;   245
My love, my life, my soul, fair Helena.

HELENA   O, excellent!

HERMIA   Sweet, do not scorn her so.

To prove his love for Helena, Lysander challenges Demetrius to a duel. Hermia hangs on Lysander's arm to try to stop him going. Lysander tries to shake her loose, saying that although he hates her, he won't harm her. Hermia says hate is the worst harm he can do her, that nothing has really changed.

249   **Thou ... entreat** You have no more power to force me than she has to persuade

252   **that which ... thee** i.e. my life

254   **than ... do** than he possibly can

255   **withdraw ... too** come away and prove it; this is a challenge to a duel.

256   **whereto ... this?** what is all this leading to?

257   **Away, you Ethiope!** Once again the fairer complexion of Helena is preferred to the darker hair and skin of Hermia. A woman from Ethiopia would have the dark colouring of an African.

         sir, yield give in to Hermia

258   **Seem ... follow** pretend to break loose. Look as though you intend to follow

259   **tame** pathetic, feeble

260   **Hang ... loose** Get off me, wretched thing! Let go

         burr A seedhead with little hooks which will cling to clothing.

262   **rude** rough

263   **tawny Tartar** dark-skinned Asian (obviously intended as yet another term of abuse)

265   **Do you not jest?** You're surely joking

267–8   **I would ... holds you** I wish I had your pledge, for I can see a feeble tie holds you back; Demetrius is making a **pun** on the word 'bond' 1) pledge 2) tie, restraint (see Glossary p. 228).

272   **wherefore?** why?

         what news what is going on

274   **I am ... erewhile** I am as pretty now as I ever was

275   **Since ... left me** When night fell you were still in love with me but since night fell you have left me

DEMETRIUS If she cannot entreat, I can compel.

LYSANDER Thou canst compel no more than she entreat.
Thy threats have no more strength than her weak
    prayers.   250
Helen, I love thee, by my life I do.
I swear by that which I will lose for thee,
To prove him false that says I love thee not.

DEMETRIUS I say I love thee more than he can do.

LYSANDER If thou say so, withdraw and prove it too.   255

DEMETRIUS Quick, come –

HERMIA   Lysander, whereto tends all this?

LYSANDER Away, you Ethiope!

DEMETRIUS   No, no, sir, yield
Seem to break loose. Take on as you would follow,
But yet come not. You are a tame man, go!

LYSANDER Hang off thou cat, thou burr! Vile thing, let loose, 260
Or I will shake thee from me like a serpent.

HERMIA Why are you grown so rude? What change is this,
Sweet love?

LYSANDER   Thy love? Out tawny Tartar, out!
Out, loathed medicine! O hated potion, hence!

HERMIA Do you not jest?

HELENA   Yes sooth, and so do you.   265

LYSANDER Demetrius, I will keep my word with thee.

DEMETRIUS I would I had your bond, for I perceive
A weak bond holds you. I'll not trust your word.

LYSANDER What, should I hurt her, strike her, kill her dead?
Although I hate her, I'll not harm her so.   270

HERMIA What, can you do me greater harm than hate?
Hate me, wherefore? O me, what news, my love?
Am not I Hermia? Are not you Lysander?
I am as fair now as I was erewhile.
Since night you loved me; yet since night you left
    me.   275

Hermia has just made an appeal to Lysander. It does not affect him. He assures her that he wants her out of his sight for ever. He hates her and loves Helena. At this, Hermia turns on Helena, her former friend.

277	**In earnest** Seriously
282	**juggler** trickster
	canker-blossom A grub that destroys flower buds and leaves.
284	**Fine, i' faith!** Helena is sarcastic; she still thinks that Hermia has joined the men in making fun of her.
288	**counterfeit** fraud
	puppet This is one of many references to Hermia's shortness.
290–1	**Now I ... height** I see that she has compared our heights, and she's used her height to gain an advantage
292	**personage** appearance
293	**forsooth** indeed
	prevailed succeeded
294	**are you ... esteem** does he now think so much of you
295	**dwarfish** short as a dwarf
296	**painted** Hermia says Helena has used make-up to improve her complexion.
	maypole A tall decorated pole which people danced around on May 1st. The emphasis is again on Helena's height.
300	**curst** bad-tempered
301	**shrewishness** quarrelling and insulting people
302	**right** proper
304	**something lower** rather shorter
305	**can match her** would be her equal in a fight
307–8	**I evermore ... counsels** I've always been your friend, always kept your secrets

Why then, you left me – O, the gods forbid –
In earnest, shall I say?

LYSANDER   Ay, by my life.
And never did desire to see thee more.
Therefore be out of hope, of question, of doubt.
Be certain, nothing truer; 'tis no jest   280
That I do hate thee and love Helena.

HERMIA   O me, you juggler, you canker-blossom,
You thief of love. What, have you come by night
And stolen my love's heart from him?

HELENA   Fine, i' faith!
Have you no modesty, no maiden shame,   285
No touch of bashfulness? What, will you tear
Impatient answers from my gentle tongue?
Fie, fie, you counterfeit, you puppet, you!

HERMIA   Puppet? Why so? Ay, that way goes the game.
Now I perceive that she hath made compare   290
Between our statures, she hath urged her height,
And with her personage, her tall personage,
Her height, forsooth, she hath prevailed with him.
And are you grown so high in his esteem,
Because I am so dwarfish and so low?   295
How low am I, thou painted maypole? Speak;
How low am I? I am not yet so low,
But that my nails can reach unto thine eyes.

HELENA   I pray you, though you mock me, gentlemen,
Let her not hurt me. I was never curst.   300
I have no gift at all in shrewishness.
I am a right maid for my cowardice.
Let her not strike me. You perhaps may think,
Because she is something lower than myself
That I can match her.

HERMIA   Lower? Hark, again.   305

HELENA   Good Hermia, do not be so bitter with me.
I evermore did love you Hermia,
Did ever keep your counsels, never wronged you;

Helena sadly offers to leave, but the quarrel flares up again. This time the men can scarcely keep Hermia and Helena apart. The two men leave to fight the duel. It is supposed to prove which of the men is more in love with Helena.

309	**Save that** except that
	in love unto for love of
310	**your stealth** your stealing away
312	**chid me hence** told me to go away
314	**so** if
315	**folly** foolish behaviour
317	**fond** foolish
323	**keen** bitter
	shrewd sharp
327	**suffer ... thus** allow her to insult me like this
328	**come to her** get at her
329	**minimus** tiny creature
	knot-grass low-growing grass (It seems that the juice of it was given to dwarves kept as court entertainers, to stunt their growth.)
330	**officious** eager to do your duty
333–5	**For ... aby it** For if you show even the slightest amount of affection for her, you will be made to pay for it
338	**cheek by jowl** side by side

	Save that, in love unto Demetrius,
	I told him of your stealth unto this wood. 310
	He followed you; for love I followed him.
	But he hath chid me hence and threatened me
	To strike me, spurn me; nay, to kill me too.
	And now, so you will let me quiet go,
	To Athens will I bear my folly back, 315
	And follow you no further. Let me go.
	You see how simple and how fond I am.
HERMIA	Why, get you gone. Who is 't that hinders you?
HELENA	A foolish heart, that I leave here behind.
HERMIA	What with Lysander?
HELENA	With Demetrius. 320
LYSANDER	Be not afraid; he shall not harm thee Helena.
DEMETRIUS	No sir, she shall not, though you take her part.
HELENA	O, when she's angry, she is keen and shrewd.
	She was a vixen when she went to school;
	And though she be but little, she is fierce. 325
HERMIA	'Little' again? Nothing but 'low' and 'little'.
	Why will you suffer her to flout me thus?
	Let me come to her.
LYSANDER	Get you gone, you dwarf,
	You minimus, of hindering knot-grass made,
	You bead, you acorn.
DEMETRIUS	You are too officious 330
	In her behalf that scorns your services.
	Let her alone; speak not of Helena;
	Take not her part. For, if thou dost intend
	Never so little show of love to her,
	Thou shalt aby it.
LYSANDER	Now she holds me not. 335
	Now follow, if thou dar'st, to try whose right,
	Of thine or mine, is most in Helena.
DEMETRIUS	Follow? Nay, I'll go with thee, cheek by jowl.

[*Exeunt* LYSANDER *and* DEMETRIUS

Afraid of a fight with Hermia, Helena runs off. Hermia leaves too. Oberon tells Puck off for making such a bad mistake. He orders him to use magic to keep Lysander and Demetrius from fighting.

339	**coil** fuss, bother
	'long of you on account of you
341	**curst** quarrelsome, bad-tempered
342	**fray** fight
346	**committ'st ... wilfully** are doing these tricks deliberately
350	**so far ... enterprise** my venture has been blameless to the extent
352	**sort** turn out
353	**jangling** wrangling
355	**Hie** Go
356	**welkin** sky, heavens
357	**Acheron** One of the rivers of the Underworld in Greek myth.
358	**testy** short-tempered
359	**As ... way** so that they cannot meet again
360	**Like ... tongue** Sometimes imitate Lysander's speech
362	**rail** be abusive
364	**death-counterfeiting sleep** a sleep so deep it seems like death
365	**batty wings** wings like those of bats
367	**virtuous property** powerful quality
368	**take ... might** take away from his eye all the mistaken idea of love
369	**wonted sight** usual way of looking
370	**derision** ridicule
371	**fruitless vision** pointless display
372	**wend** return
373	**With ... end** as companions until death

HERMIA	You, mistress, all this coil is 'long of you.
	Nay, go not back.
HELENA	I will not trust you, I,	340
	Nor longer stay in your curst company.
	Your hands than mine are quicker for a fray,
	My legs are longer though, to run away. [*Exit*
HERMIA	I am amazed, and know not what to say. [*Exit*
OBERON	This is thy negligence. Still thou mistak'st,	345
	Or else committ'st thy knaveries wilfully.
PUCK	Believe me, king of shadows, I mistook.
	Did not you tell me I should know the man
	By the Athenian garments he had on?
	And so far blameless proves my enterprise,	350
	That I have 'nointed an Athenian's eyes;
	And so far am I glad it so did sort,
	As this their jangling I esteem a sport.
OBERON	Thou see'st these lovers seek a place to fight:
	Hie therefore Robin, overcast the night,	355
	The starry welkin cover thou anon
	With drooping fog as black as Acheron,
	And lead these testy rivals so astray,
	As one come not within another's way.
	Like to Lysander sometime frame thy tongue,	360
	Then stir Demetrius up with bitter wrong;
	And sometime rail thou like Demetrius;
	And from each other look thou lead them thus,
	Till o'er their brows death-counterfeiting sleep
	With leaden legs and batty wings doth creep.	365
	Then crush this herb into Lysander's eye,
	Whose liquor hath this virtuous property,
	To take from thence all error with his might,
	And make his eyeballs roll with wonted sight.
	When they next wake, all this derision	370
	Shall seem a dream and fruitless vision,
	And back to Athens shall the lovers wend,
	With league whose date till death shall never end.

Oberon declares that, while Puck is correcting his mistake, he will go and claim the Indian boy he wants from Titania. They will do this as quickly as possible because it will soon be dawn. The two men return and Puck starts to lead them away from one another.

374   **Whiles ... employ** While I'm using you to do this task

376–7 **I will ... view** I will free her sight from looking at this monster with love

379   **night's ... fast** The idea is that night's chariot has been drawn by dragons. They are now retreating as it is nearly dawn.

380   **Aurora's harbinger** the herald of dawn i.e. the morning star, which appears before dawn

382   **Troop ... churchyards** return to their graves (It was commonly believed that ghosts must do this as day dawned.)

383   **in crossways ... burial** buried at crossroads or still in the sea (Those who had committed suicide were damned by the Church and so their bodies could not be buried in consecrated ground.)

386–7 **They wilfully ... night** because they deliberately shut themselves off from an afterlife in the light, they have to keep company with night for ever

388   **another sort** a different kind

389   **I with ... sport** I have often enjoyed Aurora's love (He is making it clear that he doesn't have to disappear at dawn.)

390   **like ... tread** like a forest warden and gamekeeper, I can be up and about early in the day

391–3 **eastern ... streams** the red pathway over the waves, as the light changes, seems to alter the green of the sea to yellow

           Neptune the god of water

402   **drawn** with my sword drawn (Puck is leading the two men apart.)

404   **plainer** more level

	Whiles I in this affair do thee employ,	
	I'll to my queen, and beg her Indian boy:	375
	And then I will her charmed eye release	
	From monster's view, and all things shall be peace.	
PUCK	My fairy lord, this must be done with haste.	

PUCK   My fairy lord, this must be done with haste.
For night's swift dragons cut the clouds full fast,
And yonder shines Aurora's harbinger;   380
At whose approach, ghosts, wandering here and
        there,
Troop home to churchyards; damned spirits all,
That in crossways and floods have burial,
Already to their wormy beds are gone;
For fear lest day should look their shames upon,   385
They wilfully themselves exile from light,
And must for aye consort with black-browed night.

OBERON But we are spirits of another sort.
I with the morning's love have oft made sport,
And like a forester the groves may tread,   390
Even till the eastern gate, all fiery-red,
Opening on Neptune with fair blessed beams,
Turns into yellow gold his salt green streams.
But notwithstanding, haste, make no delay:
We may effect this business yet ere day.   395

                                              [*Exit*

PUCK   Up and down, up and down,
I will lead them up and down
I am feared in field and town.
Goblin, lead them up and down.
Here comes one.   400

        Enter LYSANDER

LYSANDER Where art thou, proud Demetrius? Speak thou now.

PUCK   Here villain, drawn and ready! Where art thou?

LYSANDER I will be with thee straight.

PUCK   Follow me then
          To plainer ground.   [*Exit* LYSANDER *following the voice*

Puck leads Lysander and Demetrius all over the place, until they separately lie down to sleep. Then Demetrius decides to wait until daylight to find and fight his enemy.

405	**art thou fled?** have you run away?
407	**bragging** boasting
408–9	**Telling ... come?** are you pretending loudly that you want a fight but won't show yourself?
409	**recreant** coward
410	**defiled** shamed, dirtied
417	**That ... way** I have come upon a rough, dark place
422	**Abide me** Wait for me (Puck now gives Demetrius the treatment.)
	well I wot I know very well
426	**Thou ... dear** You'll pay a heavy price for this

Enter DEMETRIUS

DEMETRIUS	Lysander, speak again.

Thou runaway, thou coward, art thou fled?   405
Speak! In some bush? Where dost thou hide thy
    head?

PUCK   Thou coward, art thou bragging to the stars,
Telling the bushes that thou look'st for wars.
And wilt not come? Come recreant, come thou
    child,
I'll whip thee with a rod. He is defiled   410
That draws a sword on thee.

DEMETRIUS   Yea, art thou there?

PUCK   Follow my voice, we'll try no manhood here.

                                     [*Exeunt*

Enter LYSANDER

LYSANDER   He goes before me, and still dares me on.
When I come where he calls, then he is gone.
The villain is much lighter-heeled than I,   415
I followed fast, but faster he did fly;
That fallen am I in dark uneven way,
And here will rest me. [*Lies down*] Come thou
    gentle day,
For if but once thou show me thy grey light,
I'll find Demetrius and revenge this spite. [*Sleeps* 420

Enter PUCK *and* DEMETRIUS

PUCK   Ho, ho, ho! Coward, why comest thou not?

DEMETRIUS Abide me if thou dar'st, for well I wot
Thou runn'st before me, shifting every place,
And darest not stand, nor look me in the face.
Where art thou now?

PUCK   Come hither; I am here.   425

DEMETRIUS Nay then, thou mock'st me. Thou shalt buy this
    dear,
If ever I thy face by daylight see.

Helena comes to the same place as the men. She does not see them in the darkness and lies down to sleep. Shortly afterwards Hermia comes along. She is exhausted, and goes to sleep, hoping that Lysander will come to no harm. Puck puts the juice on Lysander's eyes, so that he will fall in love again with the woman he really loves.

428   **constraineth** forces

429   **measure ... length** lie down

430   **By day's ... visited** Expect to see me coming when it's daylight

432   **Abate** shorten

435   **sometimes ... eye** sometimes sleep can bring comfort to sorrow

439   **curst** cross

440   **knavish** wicked

443   **Bedabbled** sprinkled

445   **My legs ... desires** my legs don't obey me any more

447   **Heavens ... fray** May Heaven protect Lysander if they (Lysander and Demetrius) intend to fight

Now, go thy way. Faintness constraineth me
To measure out my length on this cold bed.
By day's approach look to be visited.   430

[Lies down and sleeps

Enter HELENA

HELENA O weary night, O long and tedious night,
Abate thy hours. Shine comforts from the east,
That I may back to Athens by daylight,
From these that my poor company detest.
And sleep, that sometimes shuts up sorrow's eye,   435
Steal me awhile from mine own company.

[Lies down and sleeps

PUCK Yet but three? Come one more.
Two of both kinds makes up four.
Here she comes, curst and sad.
Cupid is a knavish lad,   440
Thus to make poor females mad.

Enter HERMIA

HERMIA Never so weary, never so in woe,
Bedabbled with the dew, and torn with briers,
I can no further crawl, no further go;
My legs can keep no pace with my desires.   445
Here will I rest me till the break of day.
Heavens shield Lysander, if they mean a fray.

[Lies down and sleeps

PUCK On the ground
Sleep sound;
I'll apply   450
To your eye
Gentle lover, remedy.

[Puts the juice on Lysander's eyes

When thou wak'st,
Thou tak'st
True delight   455
In the sight

Puck says that everything will be all right.

461   **Jack ... Jill** the man shall have his girl

463   **The man ... again** Puck uses proverbs to tell us that all will end happily.

Act 3 scene 2
Recap: the lovers
Work on your own

Remind yourself of the situation at the beginning of this scene. Copy the diagram below and draw arrows to show who loves whom.

Of thy former lady's eye.
And the country proverb known,
That every man should take his own,
In your waking shall be shown.   460
Jack shall have Jill;
Nought shall go ill;
The man shall have his mare again,
And all shall be well.

[*Exit*

ACTIVITIES

Why does Oberon's plan backfire?

Work with a partner

1 Read again lines 88–99.

2 Discuss the answers to these questions:

   a Why does Oberon criticise Puck?

   b What is his new plan?

3 Now read lines 137–50.

4 Discuss the answers to these questions:

   a In what way is Oberon's plan successful?

   b In what way is it a failure?

   c So why does his plan backfire?

Tracking Helena

In the middle part of this scene our attention is focused on Helena. First she is pursued by Lysander who swears he loves her, but whom she doesn't believe. She thinks he is making fun of her by pretending to love her. Then Demetrius, who has rejected her love since the beginning of the play, wakes up from his sleep and declares he loves her!

Her mood changes throughout the scene. At times she is furious, while at others she attempts to argue reasonably. We can plot her mood changes on a graph like this:

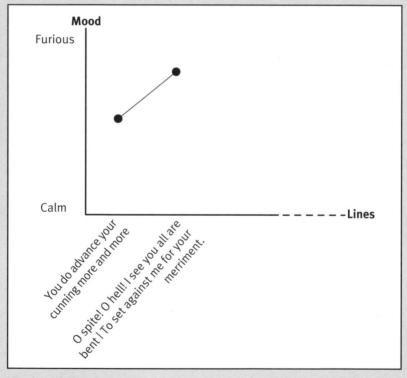

Work with a partner

Copy out the diagram onto a large sheet of paper. Plot on it how and when Helena's mood changes during the scene. For each point write a short quotation at the bottom. You should be able to plot six or seven events on your graphs.

Plot summary quiz

The ten quotations below sum up what happens in Act 3.

1 Work out the correct order for them.

2 Work out who said each one.

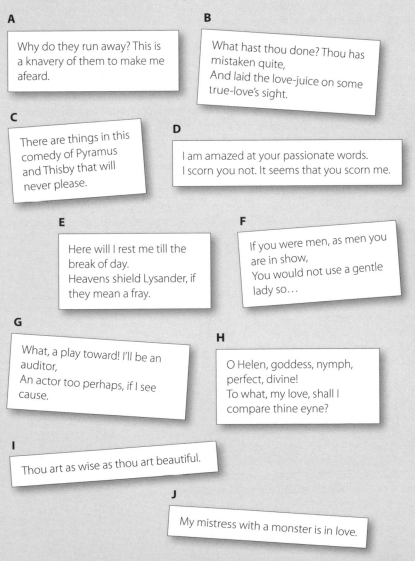

A

Why do they run away? This is a knavery of them to make me afeard.

B

What hast thou done? Thou has mistaken quite,
And laid the love-juice on some true-love's sight.

C

There are things in this comedy of Pyramus and Thisby that will never please.

D

I am amazed at your passionate words.
I scorn you not. It seems that you scorn me.

E

Here will I rest me till the break of day.
Heavens shield Lysander, if they mean a fray.

F

If you were men, as men you are in show,
You would not use a gentle lady so…

G

What, a play toward! I'll be an auditor,
An actor too perhaps, if I see cause.

H

O Helen, goddess, nymph, perfect, divine!
To what, my love, shall I compare thine eyne?

I

Thou art as wise as thou art beautiful.

J

My mistress with a monster is in love.

The four lovers are lying asleep while Oberon, also unseen, watches Titania sitting with Bottom, while her fairies wait on him.

2   **amiable ... coy** caress your lovely cheeks

8   **Monsieur** The fairies are so foreign to Bottom that he feels he must give them foreign 'titles'.

13   **fret** worry

16   **overflown with** covered in

19   **neaf** fist

20   **leave your courtesy** stop bowing (possibly because Bottom would rather shake hands)

22   **Cavalery** Another attempt by Bottom to be polite by using a word based on the Italian *cavaliere*.

Act Four

Scene ❶

The wood

LYSANDER, DEMETRIUS, HELENA, *and* HERMIA *lying asleep*

Enter TITANIA *and* BOTTOM; PEASEBLOSSOM, COBWEB, MOTH, MUSTARDSEED, *and other Fairies attending;* OBERON *behind unseen*

TITANIA	Come sit thee down upon this flowery bed,
	While I thy amiable cheeks do coy,
	And stick musk-roses in thy sleek smooth head,
	And kiss thy fair large ears, my gentle joy.
BOTTOM	Where's Peaseblossom? 5
PEASEBLOSSOM	Ready.
BOTTOM	Scratch my head, Peaseblossom. Where's Monsieur Cobweb?
COBWEB	Ready.
BOTTOM	Monsieur Cobweb, good monsieur, get you your 10 weapons in your hand, and kill me a red-hipped humble-bee on the top of a thistle; and good monsieur, bring me the honey-bag. Do not fret yourself too much in the action, monsieur; and good monsieur, have a care the honey-bag break 15 not, I would be loth to have you overflown with a honey-bag signior. Where's Monsieur Mustardseed?
MUSTARDSEED	Ready.
BOTTOM	Give me your neaf, Monsieur Mustardseed. Pray you, leave your courtsey, good monsieur. 20
MUSTARDSEED	What's your will?
BOTTOM	Nothing, good monsieur, but to help Cavalery Cobweb to scratch. I must to the barber's,

Bottom, offered music, only wants the kind he is used to; offered food he asks for the food a donkey would enjoy. He falls asleep in Titania's arms. Oberon tells Puck he is beginning to feel sorry for Titania, and tells him of his recent meeting with her.

29   **tongs ... bones** Simple musical instruments: tongs were made of metal to be hit, rather like a triangle, and bones would be held between the fingers and struck together. Bottom wants the music he's used to.

31   **peck of provender** a load of food (A peck is an old measure of volume.)

33   **bottle of hay** bundle of hay

33–4 **no fellow** no equal

36   **squirrel's hoard** Squirrels collect nuts when there are plenty and hide them away.

39   **exposition of sleep** Bottom means 'disposition' to sleep.

42   **woodbine** Sometimes seems to mean honeysuckle; sometimes, as here, convolvulus.

44   **Enrings** twines around

      barky fingers twigs

47   **dotage** foolish infatuation

48   **of late** recently

49   **favours** gifts

50   **upbraid** scold

53–6 **dew ... bewail** Oberon, noticing the dew still clinging to the flowers which Titania had used to make a garland for Bottom's head, and seeing them like tears, was angry with her.

	monsieur, for methinks I am marvellous hairy	
	about the face. And I am such a tender ass if my	25
	hair do but tickle me, I must scratch.	

TITANIA What, wilt thou hear some music, my sweet love?

BOTTOM I have a reasonable good ear in music. Let's have
the tongs and the bones.

TITANIA Or say, sweet love, what thou desirest to eat.   30

BOTTOM Truly a peck of provender. I could munch your
good dry oats. Methinks I have a great desire to a
bottle of hay. Good hay, sweet hay, hath no
fellow.

TITANIA I have a venturous fairy that shall seek   35
The squirrel's hoard, and fetch thee new nuts.

BOTTOM I had rather have a handful or two of dried peas.
But, I pray you, let none of your people stir me. I
have an exposition of sleep come upon me.

TITANIA Sleep thou, and I will wind thee in my arms.   40
Fairies be gone, and be all ways away.

[*Exeunt fairies*

So doth the woodbine, the sweet honeysuckle,
Gently entwist; the female ivy so
Enrings the barky fingers of the elm.
O, how I love thee! How I dote on thee!   45

[*They sleep*

Enter PUCK

OBERON [*Advancing*] Welcome, good Robin. See'st thou this
sweet sight?
Her dotage now I do begin to pity.
For meeting her of late behind the wood,
Seeking sweet favours for this hateful fool,
I did upbraid her and fall out with her.   50
For she his hairy temples then had rounded
With coronet of fresh and fragrant flowers.
And that same dew, which sometime on the buds
Was wont to swell like round and orient pearls,
Stood now within the pretty flowerets' eyes   55

Oberon was cross with her when he met her with Bottom. She begged his forgiveness and gave up the Indian child to him. Oberon tells Puck to take the ass's head off Bottom's head, so that all the humans can go back to Athens. He takes the magic spell off Titania. She wakes up, hating the sight of Bottom. Puck takes off the ass's head. Oberon and Titania are together again.

60   **straight** instantly

62–3   **undo ... eyes** release her eyes from this hateful distorted view

64   **transformed scalp** altered head

65   **swain** peasant

67   **repair** return

69   **fierce vexation** strong anguish

71   **wast wont to** used to

73   **Dian's ... flower** It is impossible to determine which flowers Shakespeare means. The point is that Oberon now uses a different charm to restore the influence of Diana, the goddess of chastity, over Venus and Cupid.

77   **enamoured of** in love with

81–2   **strike ... sense** The music must make Bottom and the four lovers totally unaware of what is happening.

87   **new in amity** friends again; Oberon has drugged, fooled, tormented, ridiculed and blackmailed Titania.

Like tears that did their own disgrace bewail.
When I had at my pleasure taunted her,
And she in mild terms begged my patience,
I then did ask of her her changeling child,
Which straight she gave me, and her fairy sent   60
To bear him to my bower in Fairyland.
And now I have the boy, I will undo
This hateful imperfection of her eyes.
And, gentle Puck, take this transformed scalp
From off the head of this Athenian swain;   65
That he, awaking when the other do,
May all to Athens back again repair,
And think no more of this night's accidents,
But as the fierce vexation of a dream.
But first I will release the Fairy Queen.   70
    Be as thou wast wont to be;
    See as thou wast wont to see.
    Dian's bud o'er Cupid's flower
    Hath such force and blessed power.
Now my Titania, wake you, my sweet queen.   75

TITANIA   My Oberon, what visions have I seen!
Methought I was enamoured of an ass.

OBERON   There lies your love.

TITANIA   How came these things to pass?
O, how mine eyes do loathe his visage now.

OBERON   Silence awhile. Robin, take off this head.   80
Titania, music call, and strike more dead
Than common sleep of all these five the sense.

TITANIA   Music, ho! music, such as charmeth sleep.

                             [*Music*

PUCK   Now, when thou wak'st, with thine own fool's
    eyes peep.

OBERON   Sound, music. Come my queen, take hands with
    me,   85
And rock the ground whereon these sleepers be.
Now thou and I are new in amity,

Oberon and Titania dance together and promise they will dance in Duke Theseus' palace and bless it. Puck says it will soon be dawn. They leave and Theseus, Hippolyta, Egeus and their attendants come in. They intend to hunt, and talk about hounds they have seen and heard.

94   **morning lark** The lark sings as it grows light.

96   **Trip ... shade** Follow night as it goes

97–8 **We ... moon** We can circle the world more quickly than the moon

103   **find out** look for

104   **observation** celebration of midsummer day

105   **since ... day** as it is still early in the day

106   **music** The sound the hounds make baying when on a scent.

107   **Uncouple** Let the hounds go (They have been chained in pairs.)

108   **Dispatch** Hurry

110   **mark** listen to

111   **in conjunction** together

112   **Hercules and Cadmus** Two heroes of Greek mythology.

113   **bayed the bear** hunted the bear until it was cornered and forced to turn and fight the hounds 'at bay'

115   **chiding** (here) barking angrily

119   **bred ... kind** the Spartan breed

	And will tomorrow midnight solemnly	
	Dance in Duke Theseus' house triumphantly	
	And bless it to all fair prosperity.	90
	There shall the pairs of faithful lovers be	
	Wedded, with Theseus, all in jollity.	
PUCK	Fairy King, attend, and mark,	
	I do hear the morning lark.	
OBERON	Then, my queen, in silence sad,	95
	Trip we after night's shade.	
	We the globe can compass soon,	
	Swifter than the wandering moon.	
TITANIA	Come my lord, and in our flight,	
	Tell me how it came this night	100
	That I sleeping here was found	
	With these mortals on the ground. [*Exeunt*	

[*Wind horns*

Enter THESEUS, HIPPOLYTA, EGEUS, *and train*

THESEUS	Go one of you, find out the forester;	
	For now our observation is performed,	
	And since we have the vaward of the day,	105
	My love shall hear the music of my hounds.	
	Uncouple in the western valley, let them go.	
	Dispatch I say, and find the forester.	

[*Exit an Attendant*

	We will, fair queen, up to the mountain's top,	
	And mark the musical confusion	110
	Of hounds and echo in conjunction.	
HIPPOLYTA	I was with Hercules and Cadmus once,	
	When in a wood of Crete they bayed the bear	
	With hounds of Sparta; never did I hear	
	Such gallant chiding. For, besides the groves,	115
	The skies, the fountains, every region near	
	Seemed all one mutual cry. I never heard	
	So musical a discord, such sweet thunder.	
THESEUS	My hounds are bred out of the Spartan kind,	

The talk of hounds continues until Theseus notices the lovers asleep. Egeus is surprised to see them. Theseus remembers that this is the day Hermia had to give her choice: Demetrius or the convent or death. The huntsman wakes them with the horn, and, still drowsy with sleep, Lysander tries to answer their questions.

120	**So flewed** with the same, loose-hanging skin around their jaws
	so sanded with similar sandy markings
122	**Crook-kneed** with bent legs
	dew-lapped with folds of skin around their throats
	Thessalian bulls Bulls found in Thessaly, Greece.
123	**matched in mouth** chosen for the harmonious sound of their baying
124	**Each under each** some high, some lower in pitch
125	**hollaed to** 'Halloo' is the call of the huntsman in the chase.
	horn hunting horn
127	**soft** wait a moment
	nymphs young women
131	**I wonder of** I am surprised at
133	**rite of May** i.e. the Mayday/midsummer celebrations already referred to (Act 1 scene 1 line 167 and Act 4 scene 1 line 104)
134	**in grace ... solemnity** in honour of our celebrations
139–40	**Saint ... now?** St Valentine is the patron saint of lovers and on St Valentine's day the birds were thought to choose their mates.
	couple pair up
141	**Pardon, my lord** When the lovers wake up and realise this is the Duke, they all kneel. They get up again when Theseus instructs them to (line 141).
144	**jealousy** suspicion
145	**by hate** beside a person who hates you
146	**amazedly** in confusion
150	**do bethink me** come to think about it

	So flewed, so sanded, and their heads are hung	120
	With ears that sweep away the morning dew,
	Crook-kneed and dew-lapped like Thessalian bulls;
	Slow in pursuit, but matched in mouth like bells,
	Each under each. A cry more tuneable
	Was never hollaed to, nor cheered with horn,	125
	In Crete, in Sparta, nor in Thessaly.
	Judge when you hear. But soft, what nymphs are these?

EGEUS   My lord, this is my daughter here asleep,
          And this, Lysander, this Demetrius is,
          This Helena, old Nedar's Helena.   130
          I wonder of their being here together.

THESEUS   No doubt they rose up early to observe
          The rite of May; and hearing our intent,
          Came here in grace of our solemnity.
          But speak, Egeus, is not this the day   135
          That Hermia should give answer of her choice?

EGEUS   It is, my lord.

THESEUS   Go bid the huntsmen wake them with their horns.

                    [*Wind horns. Shout within. They all start up*

          Good morrow, friends. Saint Valentine is past.
          Begin these wood-birds but to couple now?   140

LYSANDER Pardon, my lord.

THESEUS   I pray you all, stand up.
          I know you two are rival enemies.
          How comes this gentle concord in the world,
          That hatred is so far from jealousy,
          To sleep by hate, and fear no enmity?   145

LYSANDER My lord, I shall reply amazedly,
          Half sleep, half waking. But as yet, I swear,
          I cannot truly say how I came here.
          But as I think – for truly would I speak,
          And now I do bethink me, so it is –   150
          I came with Hermia hither. Our intent
          Was to be gone from Athens, where we might

The minute Lysander mentions 'Athenian law' Egeus breaks in. He demands that the law deal with him, for taking his daughter away. Demetrius steps in, explaining that Helena now has his love again, and promising it will be for ever. Theseus overrules Egeus and promises a triple wedding.

160	**stealth** stealing away secretly
161	**purpose hither** intention to come here
163	**in fancy** because of love
164	**I wot not** I do not know
167	**remembrance ... gaud** memory of a useless toy
168	**did dote upon** was foolishly fond of
169	**all ... heart** all that my heart sees faith and value in
173	**like a sickness** as though I were ill
178	**discourse** talk
	anon later
179	**overbear your will** overrule your wishes
181	**eternally be knit** be married
182	**for the ... worn** as it is now quite late
183	**Our ... aside** the hunting we proposed to do shall be abandoned
184	**three and three** three men, three women
185	**solemnity** celebrations

Without the peril of the Athenian law –

EGEUS   Enough, enough, my lord, you have enough:
I beg the law, the law, upon his head.   155
They would have stolen away, they would,
        Demetrius,
Thereby to have defeated you and me,
You of your wife, and me of my consent,
Of my consent that she should be your wife.

DEMETRIUS My lord, fair Helen told me of their stealth,   160
Of this their purpose hither to this wood;
And I in fury hither followed them,
Fair Helena in fancy following me.
But, my good lord, I wot not by what power –
But by some power it is – my love to Hermia,   165
Melted as the snow, seems to me now
As the remembrance of an idle gaud,
Which in my childhood I did dote upon.
And all the faith, the virtue of my heart,
The object and the pleasure of mine eye,   170
Is only Helena. To her, my lord,
Was I betrothed ere I saw Hermia;
But, like a sickness, did I loathe this food;
But, as in health, come to my natural taste,
Now I do wish it, love it, long for it,   175
And will for evermore be true to it.

THESEUS Fair lovers, you are fortunately met.
Of this discourse we more will hear anon.
Egeus, I will overbear your will;
For in the temple, by and by, with us   180
These couples shall eternally be knit.
And, for the morning now is something worn,
Our purposed hunting shall be set aside.
Away with us to Athens, three and three,
We'll hold a feast in great solemnity.   185
Come Hippolyta.

[*Exeunt* THESEUS, HIPPOLYTA, EGEUS, *and train*

The court and courtiers leave and the four lovers, still in a dream, start to try and work out what has happened. They follow the duke's party. Bottom, in his turn, wakes up still half-remembering the marvels he has experienced. He feels it should be written down as it is both unique and deep. He would like to call it 'Bottom's Dream' and perform it at the end of their play.

189   **parted eye** double vision, unfocused eyes

192   **Mine own ... mine own** The idea is that if you find something it feels as though it is yours, but it doesn't necessarily belong to you.

194   **yet** still

199   **recount** tell

200   **cue** Bottom wakes up thinking he's still at the rehearsal.

207   **expound** explain

209   **patched fool** a jester or court fool in patchwork clothes

210–14 **The eye ... dream was** Bottom is left in a very confused state, as the language suggests.

214   **ballad** popular song

216   **hath no bottom** is unfathomable, has no rational explanation

217   **Peradventure** Perhaps

218   **her death** i.e. Thisby's death

DEMETRIUS   These things seem small and undistinguishable,
Like far-off mountains turned into clouds.

HERMIA   Methinks I see these things with parted eye,
When everything seems double.

HELENA   So methinks.   190
And I have found Demetrius like a jewel,
Mine own, and not mine own.

DEMETRIUS   Are you sure
That we are awake? It seems to me
That yet we sleep, we dream. Do not you think
The duke was here, and bid us follow him?   195

HERMIA   Yea, and my father.

HELENA   And Hippolyta.

LYSANDER   And he did bid us follow to the temple.

DEMETRIUS   Why then we are awake, let's follow him.
And by the way let us recount our dreams.

[Exeunt

BOTTOM   [*Awaking*] When my cue comes, call me, and I   200
will answer. My next is, 'Most fair Pyramus'. Heigh-
ho. Peter Quince! Flute the bellows-mender!
Snout the tinker! Starveling! God's my life, stolen
hence, and left me asleep. I have had a most rare
vision. I have had a dream, past the wit of man to   205
say what dream it was. Man is but an ass, if he go
about to expound this dream. Methought I was –
there is no man can tell what. Methought I was, and
methought I had – but man is but a patched fool, if
he will offer to say what methought I had. The eye   210
of man hath not heard, the ear of man hath not
seen, man's hand is not able to taste, his tongue to
conceive, nor his heart to report, what my dream
was. I will get Peter Quince to write a ballad of this
dream; it shall be called Bottom's Dream, because it   215
hath no bottom; and I will sing it in the latter end
of a play, before the duke. Peradventure, to make
it the more gracious, I shall sing it at her death.

[Exit

Bottom's four friends have been looking for him without success. They are very despondent because without him there will not be a play. They are also regretting the loss of the money the duke might have given them. Suddenly Bottom arrives.

4	**transported**	carried away, kidnapped
5	**marred**	spoiled
5–6	**goes not forward**	can't be performed
8	**discharge**	play the part of
9	**wit**	brain
11	**best person**	most suitable figure
12	**paramour**	lover
13	**paragon**	pattern of excellence
14	**thing of naught**	a shameful thing
17	**If our … forward**	If our play had gone ahead
17–18	**we had … men**	our fortunes would have been made.
19–20	**Thus … life**	Snug is suggesting that the Duke would have been so taken with Bottom's performance that he would have granted him a life-pension of sixpence a day. This would have been more than he could have earned at his trade.
21	**'scaped**	failed to receive
26	**courageous**	splendid

Scene ❷

Quince's house

Enter QUINCE, FLUTE, SNOUT, *and* STARVELING

QUINCE   Have you sent to Bottom's house? Is he come
           home yet?

STARVELING He cannot be heard of. Out of doubt he is
           transported.

FLUTE   If he come not, then the play is marred. It goes   5
           not forward, doth it?

QUINCE   It is not possible. You have not a man in all
           Athens able to discharge Pyramus but he.

FLUTE   No, he hath simply the best wit of any handicraft
           man in Athens.   10

QUINCE   Yea, and the best person too; and he is a very
           paramour for a sweet voice.

FLUTE   You must say 'paragon'. A paramour is, God
           bless us, a thing of naught.

           Enter SNUG

SNUG   Masters, the duke is coming from the temple,   15
           and there is two or three lords and ladies more
           married. If our sport had gone forward, we had
           all been made men.

FLUTE   O sweet bully Bottom. Thus hath he lost
           sixpence a day during his life; he could not have   20
           'scaped sixpence a day. An the duke had not
           given him sixpence a day for playing Pyramus,
           I'll be hanged. He would have deserved it.
           Sixpence a day in Pyramus, or nothing.

           Enter BOTTOM

BOTTOM   Where are these lads? Where are these hearts?   25

QUINCE   Bottom! O most courageous day! O, most happy
           hour!

Bottom promises to tell them what happened, but for the moment the play is the important thing. They must hurry and get ready.

28   **discourse** tell, speak of

30–1   **right ... out** exactly as it happened

34   **apparel** costumes

35   **strings** strings to tie false beards on with

36   **pumps** dancing shoes

       presently straight away

38   **preferred** short-listed

40   **pare** cut, file

BOTTOM   Masters, I am to discourse wonders. But ask me
          not what; for if I tell you, I am not true
          Athenian. I will tell you every thing, right as it   30
          fell out.

QUINCE   Let us hear, sweet Bottom.

BOTTOM   Not a word of me. All that I will tell you is, that
          the duke hath dined. Get your apparel together,
          good strings to your beards, new ribbons to your   35
          pumps, meet presently at the palace, every man
          look o'er his part. For the short and the long is,
          our play is preferred. In any case let Thisby have
          clean linen; and let not him that plays the lion
          pare his nails, for they shall hang out for the   40
          lion's claws. And most dear actors, eat no onions
          nor garlic, for we are to utter sweet breath; and I
          do not doubt but to hear them say, it is a sweet
          comedy. No more words. Away, go away!

                                                    [*Exeunt*

Act 4 scenes 1 and 2

Plot lines

In Act 3 scene 2, all the plots seem as tangled as they could possibly be. By the end of the next scene, Act 4 scene 1, everything has been sorted out. We can disentangle all this by adding to the plot lines table we started at the end of Act 1:

Plot line 1: **Theseus and Hippolyta**	Plot line 2: **The young lovers**	Plot line 3: **Bottom and his friends**	Plot line 4: **Oberon and Titania**

Work with a partner

1   Get the plot lines table you made earlier (or make a new one).

2   Below there is a list of new plot points. As before, they are in the wrong order. Put them in the table in the right order. This part of the table has been started for you:

	Demetrius has fallen in love with Hermia.	Bottom has an ass's head, and Titania has fallen in love with him.	Puck tells Oberon that Titania has fallen in love with an ass.

Plot points

- Oberon has persuaded Titania to let him have the 'changeling child', and while she is asleep with Bottom, he removes the spell.

- Bottom wakes up and is himself again. He goes off to find his companions.

- Oberon orders Puck to put everything right with the lovers.

- Puck removes the ass's head from Bottom.

- Helena says that Lysander, Demetrius, and Hermia are all making fun of her.

- While Demetrius is asleep Oberon squeezes love juice on his eyes.
- Theseus, Hippolyta, and Egeus find the lovers asleep in the forest.
- Demetrius wakes up, sees Helena, and falls in love with her.
- Theseus says that Lysander shall marry Hermia and Demetrius shall marry Helena.
- Egeus demands that Lysander be punished.
- The four lovers are led a merry dance by Puck and eventually all fall asleep, exhausted.
- Lysander and Demetrius go off to fight for Helena's love.
- The lovers awake and explain how Lysander is in love with Hermia and Demetrius is in love with Helena.
- Titania awakes and is in love with Oberon again.

Performance

Act 4 scene 1 is complicated. There are a lot of characters on stage and a lot happens. It is interesting to work out how this scene might have been staged in Shakespeare's time. There is a description of what Shakespeare's theatre was like on pages 19–22. Look at that and the pictures, and compare them with the plan of the stage and the audience area below. Think about how the scene might have been performed.

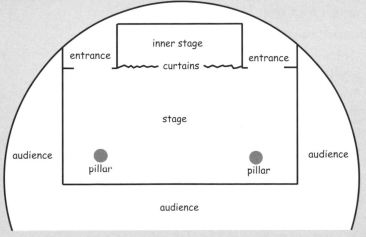

Lines 127–41

Work on your own

1 Read these lines through and try to visualise what they might have looked like in Shakespeare's theatre.

Work in a group of four

2 Take a large sheet of paper and draw a copy of the diagram on page 159. Mark on it where all the characters are at the beginning of line 127. Think about these points:

   a Whereabouts on the stage are the four lovers, and how are they arranged as they sleep?

   b Where are Theseus, Hippolyta, and Egeus when they find them?

   c Where is Bottom?

3 Now think about how the characters behave in lines 127–41. Think especially about these points:

   a How does Theseus react to seeing the lovers asleep on the ground?

   b And Egeus?

   c How do the lovers respond when they wake up and see who is looking at them?

4 Write down the names of all seven characters and for each one, write a short sentence summing up how they react.

Join up with another group

5 Cast the parts, and discuss the ideas you have developed about how the characters react to each other.

6 Read the lines sitting down. Concentrate on getting the characters' reactions right.

7 Now try the extract out with movements.

8 Discuss how it went and, if necessary, try it again until you are happy with the interpretation.

Follow-up

If time allows, follow a similar process for lines 142–81.

Quotation quiz

All these quotations come from Act 4. For each one, work out:

1 who said it

2 who they were speaking to

3 what it tells us about:

   a the speaker

   b the situation

   c any other characters.

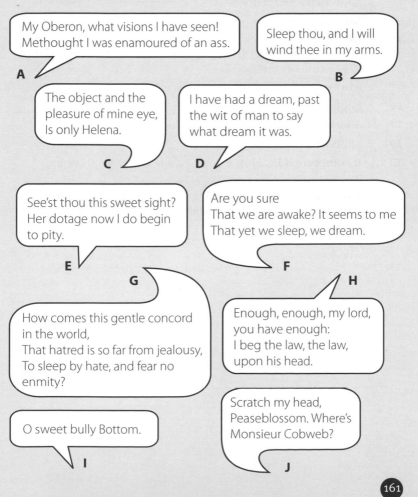

A My Oberon, what visions I have seen! Methought I was enamoured of an ass.

B Sleep thou, and I will wind thee in my arms.

C The object and the pleasure of mine eye, Is only Helena.

D I have had a dream, past the wit of man to say what dream it was.

E See'st thou this sweet sight? Her dotage now I do begin to pity.

F Are you sure That we are awake? It seems to me That yet we sleep, we dream.

G How comes this gentle concord in the world, That hatred is so far from jealousy, To sleep by hate, and fear no enmity?

H Enough, enough, my lord, you have enough: I beg the law, the law, upon his head.

I O sweet bully Bottom.

J Scratch my head, Peaseblossom. Where's Monsieur Cobweb?

Hippolyta and Theseus talk over what they have learned of the lovers' experiences in the wood. Theseus is inclined to put it all down to imagination. This affects madmen, lovers and poets, all in different ways. But Hippolyta believes there is truth in what they say, as they all tell much the same story.

3	**antique fables** old tales
	fairy toys foolish stories about fairies
4	**seething** boiling
5	**shaping fantasies** creative imaginations
	apprehend dream up
8	**Are … compact** are completely made up of imagination
11	**Helen** Famous for her beauty. When she was carried off to Troy by Paris, Priam's son, her husband Menelaus and his allies laid siege to the city for 10 years.
	a brow of Egypt a dark-skinned face like that of a gypsy
14	**bodies forth** gives mental shape to
17	**A local habitation** a real place to live
19	**apprehend** conjure up
20	**It comprehends … joy** it must include an imagined bringer of that joy
23–7	**But … admirable** But when we look at the whole story of the night's events and the fact that all their minds were affected in an identical way, it points to more than mere imagination and becomes a certainty; but still strange and something to be wondered at

Act Five

Scene ❶

THESEUS' *court*

Enter THESEUS, HIPPOLYTA, PHILOSTRATE, *Lords and Attendants*

HIPPOLYTA 'Tis strange, my Theseus, that these lovers
    speak of.

THESEUS More strange than true. I never may believe
These antique fables nor these fairy toys.
Lovers and madmen have such seething brains,
Such shaping fantasies, that apprehend   5
More than cool reason ever comprehends.
The lunatic, the lover, and the poet
Are of imagination all compact.
One sees more devils than vast hell can hold,
That is the madman. The lover, all as frantic,   10
Sees Helen's beauty in a brow of Egypt.
The poet's eye, in a fine frenzy rolling,
Doth glance from heaven to earth, from earth to
    heaven;
And as imagination bodies forth
The forms of things unknown, the poet's pen   15
Turns them to shapes, and gives to airy nothing
A local habitation and a name.
Such tricks hath strong imagination,
That if it would but apprehend some joy,
It comprehends some bringer of that joy;   20
Or in the night, imagining some fear,
How easy is a bush supposed a bear!

HIPPOLYTA But all the story of the night told over,
And all their minds transfigured so together,
More witnesseth than fancy's images,   25
And grows to something of great constancy;

The happy lovers come in. The weddings have taken place and the duke now wants to choose a suitable entertainment for the evening. Philostrate, who has organised a list of possible performances, hands it to Theseus. He has some reason for rejecting everything on the list until he comes to the title of the workmen's play.

30–1   **More … Wait** May your kind wishes for us attend you

32   **masques** entertainments

33   **wear away** pass the time during

34   **after-supper** late supper

35   **manager of mirth** Master of the Revels

36   **What … hand?** What festivities are available?

39   **abridgement** pastime

40   **beguile** pass pleasantly

          lazy slow-moving

42   **brief** summary, short list

          sports amusements

          ripe ready to be performed

44   **Centaurs** In Greek myth (see Glossary p. 227), a race of creatures with the body and legs of a horse and the chest, head and arms of a man. They were once invited to a royal wedding feast and tried to make off with the women, but were beaten and driven off.

48   **Bacchanals** These were rather wild women who followed the religious rites of the god Dionysus. The story goes that in a drunken orgy they tore the poet Orpheus to pieces.

50   **device** production

52   **Muses** In Greek myth daughters of Zeus, and goddesses of literature, music and dance and later of learning.

54   **satire** A work in prose or verse which brings ridicule on some person or thing.

55   **Not sorting with** not suitable for

But howsoever, strange and admirable.

THESEUS   Here come the lovers, full of joy and mirth.

Enter LYSANDER, DEMETRIUS, HERMIA, *and* HELENA

Joy, gentle friends, joy and fresh days of love
Accompany your hearts!

LYSANDER   More than to us   30
Wait in your royal walks, your board, your bed.

THESEUS   Come now; what masques, what dances shall we
           have,
           To wear away this long age of three hours
           Between our after-supper and bed-time?
           Where is our usual manager of mirth?   35
           What revels are in hand? Is there no play,
           To ease the anguish of a torturing hour?
           Call Philostrate.

PHILOSTRATE   Here mighty Theseus.

THESEUS   Say, what abridgement have you for this evening?
           What masque, what music? How shall we beguile   40
           The lazy time, if not with some delight?

PHILOS.   There is a brief how many sports are ripe.
           Make choice of which your highness will see first.

                                          [*Gives a paper*

THESEUS   'The battle with the Centaurs, to be sung
           By an Athenian eunuch to the harp.'   45
           We'll none of that. That have I told my love,
           In glory of my kinsman Hercules.
           'The riot of the tipsy Bacchanals,
           Tearing the Thracian singer in their rage.'
           That is an old device, and it was played   50
           When I from Thebes came last a conqueror.
           'The thrice three Muses mourning for the death
           Of learning, late deceased in beggary.'
           That is some satire, keen and critical,
           Not sorting with a nuptial ceremony.   55
           'A tedious brief scene of young Pyramus

Philostrate agrees with the description 'tedious and brief' and explains that the play is being put on by men who have never put on a performance before. He is concerned that their audience will find it comic instead of tragic. However, this is the play Theseus wants to see, and even Hippolyta's fears cannot put him off.

60	**concord** harmony, agreement
72	**Hard-handed men** artisans
74	**toiled** worked hard at
	unbreathed unpractised, inexperienced
75	**against your nuptial** with your wedding celebration in mind
79	**sport** amusement
80	**Extremely ... pain** strained to the utmost and learned by heart so painfully
82	**amiss** wrong
83	**simpleness** innocence
85	**wretchedness** lack of ability
	o'ercharged overburdened; Hippolyta is afraid she will see these men who are below her socially and intellectually doing something far too ambitious which will mean that they will fail in their attempt to please the duke.

And his love Thisby: very tragical mirth.'
Merry and tragical? Tedious and brief?
That is, hot ice and wondrous strange snow.
How shall we find the concord of this discord?   60

PHILOS. A play there is, my lord, some ten words long,
Which is as brief as I have known a play;
But by ten words, my lord, it is too long,
Which makes it tedious. For in all the play
There is not one word apt, one player fitted.   65
And tragical, my noble lord, it is;
For Pyramus therein doth kill himself.
Which when I saw rehearsed, I must confess,
Made mine eyes water.But more merry tears
The passion of loud laughter never shed.   70

THESEUS What are they that do play it?

PHILOS. Hard-handed men, that work in Athens here,
Which never laboured in their minds till now;
And now have toiled their unbreathed memories
With this same play, against your nuptial.   75

THESEUS And we will hear it.

PHILOS.   No, my noble lord –
It is not for you. I have heard it over,
And it is nothing, nothing in the world;
Unless you can find sport in their intents,
Extremely stretched and conned with cruel pain,   80
To do you service.

THESEUS   I will hear that play.
For never anything can be amiss
When simpleness and duty tender it.
Go, bring them in, and take your places, ladies.

[*Exit* PHILOSTRATE

HIPPOLYTA I love not to see wretchedness o'ercharged,   85
And duty in his service perishing.

THESEUS Why gentle sweet, you shall see no such thing.

HIPPOLYTA He says they can do nothing in this kind.

Theseus has often had to listen to speeches of welcome from people who have rehearsed them thoroughly. Then they often suffer so much from stage fright that they cannot deliver them properly. He was still content to accept their efforts as a welcome, and will be happy to do so again. The play begins with a prologue spoken by Quince. It is wrongly punctuated, and so often says the opposite of what it means.

89	**The kinder we** Then we shall be all the more generous
90	**sport** entertainment
	take ... mistake understand what they misunderstand
92	**might, not merit** their intentions rather than their achievement
93	**clerks** scholars
	purposed planned
94	**premeditated welcomes** well-prepared speeches of welcome
96	**Make ... sentences** put full stops in the middle of sentences
102	**rattling** chattering
103	**saucy** impertinent
	audacious bold
105	**to my capacity** as far as I am concerned
106	**addressed** ready to begin
112	**in despite** against your wishes
113	**minding** meaning
118	**stand upon points** bother about punctuation
119	**rid** 1) got rid of 2) ridden: a **pun** on the word 'rid' (see Glossary p. 228)
120	**stop** 1) the horse coming to a halt 2) full stop: another **pun**

THESEUS   The kinder we, to give them thanks for nothing.
               Our sport shall be take what they mistake;   90
               And what poor duty cannot do, noble respect
               Takes it in might, not merit.
               Where I have come, great clerks have purposed
               To greet me with premeditated welcomes;
               Where I have seen them shiver and look pale,   95
               Make periods in the midst of sentences,
               Throttle their practised accent in their fears,
               And in conclusion dumbly have broke off,
               Not paying me a welcome. Trust me sweet,
               Out of this silence yet I picked a welcome;   100
               And in the modesty of fearful duty
               I read as much as from the rattling tongue
               Of saucy and audacious eloquence.
               Love, therefore, and tongue-tied simplicity
               In least speak most, to my capacity.   105

               Enter PHILOSTRATE

PHILOS.   So please your grace, the prologue is addressed.

THESEUS   Let him approach.   *[Flourish of trumpets*

               Enter QUINCE *as* PROLOGUE

PROLOGUE   If we offend, it is with our good will.
               That you should think, we come not to offend,
               But with good will. To show our simple skill,   110
               That is the true beginning of our end.
               Consider then, we come but in despite.
               We do not come, as minding to content you,
               Our true intent is. All for your delight
               We are not here. That you should here repent you,   115
               The actors are at hand; and by their show,
               You shall know all, that you are like to know.

THESEUS   This fellow doth not stand upon points.

LYSANDER   He hath rid his prologue like a rough colt; he
               knows not the stop. A good moral, my lord: it is   120

The duke and duchess comment on the prologue which continues by telling the story of the whole play, indicating who is to play each character.

121	**true** properly
123	**in government** under control
125	**impaired** damaged

126–337	In the workmen's play the speakers are given the names of the characters they play:
	PROLOGUE acted by QUINCE
	WALL acted by SNOUT
	PYRAMUS acted by BOTTOM
	THISBY acted by FLUTE
	LION acted by SNUG
	MOONSHINE acted by STARVELING

126	**Gentles** Ladies and gentlemen
	perchance perhaps
131	**sunder** separate, keep apart
138	**hight** is called
141	**mantle** cloak
	fall let fall, drop
143	**tall** handsome
146	**broached** pierced
147	**tarrying** waiting
150	**At large discourse** speak at length

not enough to speak, but to speak true.

HIPPOLYTA Indeed he hath played on his prologue like a child
on a recorder, a sound, but not in government.

THESEUS His speech was like a tangled chain; nothing
impaired, but all disordered. Who is next?   125

Enter PYRAMUS *and* THISBY, WALL, MOONSHINE, *and* LION

PROLOGUE Gentles, perchance you wonder at this show,
    But wonder on, till truth make all things plain.
This man is Pyramus, if you would know;
    This beauteous lady Thisby is certain.
This man, with lime and rough-cast, doth present   130
    Wall, that vile Wall which did these lovers
        sunder,
And through Wall's chink, poor souls, they are
      content
    To whisper. At the which let no man wonder.
This man, with lanthorn, dog, and bush of thorn,
    Presenteth Moonshine. For, if you will know,   135
By moonshine did these lovers think no scorn
    To meet at Ninus' tomb, there, there to woo.
This grisly beast, which Lion hight by name,
The trusty Thisby, coming first by night,
Did scare away, or rather did affright.   140
And as she fled, her mantle she did fall,
    Which Lion vile with bloody mouth did stain.
Anon comes Pyramus, sweet youth, and tall,
    And finds his trusty Thisby's mantle slain.
Whereat, with blade, with bloody blameful blade,   145
    He bravely broached his boiling bloody breast.
And Thisby, tarrying in mulberry shade,
    His dagger drew, and died. For all the rest,
Let Lion, Moonshine, Wall, and lovers twain
At large discourse, while here they do remain.   150

[*Exeunt* PROLOGUE, PYRAMUS, THISBY, LION, *and*
                       MOONSHINE

Snout, playing the wall, explains his part. Bottom, as Pyramus, speaks first to the night, and then to the wall.

154   **interlude** play

        befall happen

160   **loam ... rough-cast ... stone** See note on p. 94, lines 64–5. Snout now seems to have added stone to his costume.

162   **sinister** left

164   **hair** Horse hair would be added to the mix to help bind the plaster to the wall.

165   **wittiest partition** most intelligent wall

176   **Jove shield thee** May God protect you

THESEUS   I wonder if the lion be to speak.

DEMETRIUS   No wonder, my lord. One lion may, when many
            asses do.

WALL   In this same interlude it doth befall
            That I, one Snout by name, present a wall;   155
            And such a wall, as I would have you think,
            That had in it a crannied hole or chink,
            Through which the lovers, Pyramus and Thisby,
            Did whisper often very secretly.
            This loam, this rough-cast, and this stone doth
               show   160
            That I am that same wall; the truth is so.
            And this the cranny is, right and sinister,
            Through which the fearful lovers are to whisper.

THESEUS   Would you desire lime and hair to speak better?

DEMETRIUS   It is the wittiest partition, that ever I heard 165
            discourse, my lord.

            Enter PYRAMUS

THESEUS   Pyramus draws near the wall: silence!

PYRAMUS   O grim-looked night! O night with hue so black!
               O night, which ever art when day is not!
            O night, O night, alack, alack, alack,   170
               I fear my Thisby's promise is forgot!
            And thou, O wall, O sweet, O lovely wall,
               That stand'st between her father's ground and
                  mine!
            Thou wall, O wall, O sweet and lovely wall,
               Show me thy chink, to blink through with mine
                  eyne!   175
                              [WALL *holds up his fingers*
            Thanks, courteous wall. Jove shield thee well for
               this.
            But what see I? No Thisby do I see.
            O wicked wall, through whom I see no bliss,
               Cursed be thy stones for thus deceiving me!

Bottom corrects the duke when he jokingly makes a comment on the play. Thisby and Pyramus declare their love through the chink in the wall. The lovers and the duke and duchess continue to comment.

180 **sensible** able to have feelings

182–4 **No ... wall** Bottom comes out of character and speaks to his audience.

184–5 **fall pat** turn out exactly

194 **Limander** Bottom means Leander, who in the Greek myth was drowned trying to swim the Hellespont to reach his love, Hero.

195 **Helen** Used mistakenly for Hero.

Fates The three sisters who in Greek mythology control our birth, life and death.

197 **as Shafalus to Procrus** A mistake for another pair of tragic lovers, Cephalus and Procris.

200 **Ninny's tomb** See note on Act 3 scene 1 line 92. Bottom is still saying 'Ninny's' for 'Ninus'.

201 **'Tide life, 'tide death** Come life, come death

202 **discharged** carried out, performed

204 **mural** wall

206 **No remedy** There is nothing to be done

209 **in this kind** i.e. actors

210 **amend them** improve on them

THESEUS	The wall methinks, being sensible, should curse	180
	again.	
BOTTOM	No in truth, sir, he should not. 'Deceiving me' is	
	Thisby's cue. She is to enter now, and I am to	
	spy her through the wall. You shall see it will fall	
	pat as I told you. Yonder she comes.	185

Enter THISBY

THISBY	O wall, full often hast thou heard my moans,	
	For parting my fair Pyramus and me!	
	My cherry lips have often kissed thy stones,	
	Thy stones with lime and hair knit up in thee.	
PYRAMUS	I see a voice; now will I to the chink,	190
	To spy an I can hear my Thisby's face.	
	Thisby!	
THISBY	My love thou art my love, I think.	
PYRAMUS	Think what thou wilt, I am thy lover's grace,	
	And, like Limander, am I trusty still.	
THISBY	And I like Helen, till the Fates me kill.	195
PYRAMUS	Not Shafalus to Procrus was so true.	
THISBY	As Shafalus to Procrus, I to you.	
PYRAMUS	O kiss me through the hole of this vile wall.	
THISBY	I kiss the wall's hole, not your lips at all.	
PYRAMUS	Wilt thou at Ninny's tomb meet me straightway?	200
THISBY	'Tide life, 'tide death, I come without delay.	

[*Exeunt* PYRAMUS *and* THISBY

WALL	Thus have I, Wall, my part discharged so;	
	And, being done, thus Wall away doth go. [*Exit*	
THESEUS	Now is the mural down between the two	
	neighbours.	205
DEMETRIUS	No remedy my lord, when walls are so wilful, to	
	hear without warning.	
HIPPOLYTA	This is the silliest stuff that ever I heard.	
THESEUS	The best in this kind are but shadows; and the	
	worst are no worse, if imagination amend them.	210

175

The lion and the moon enter and explain themselves to the audience as planned. The members of the audience make witty comments to one another.

217   **perchance** perhaps

220   **fell** 1) fierce 2) lion skin

       dam mother (Snug must be a male, not a female lion!)

221   **in strife** aggressively

222   **'twere ... life** my life would be at risk

223   **good conscience** sound judgement

225   **valour** bravery (Foxes are known for their slyness or cunning rather than bravery.)

226   **discretion** sound judgement (Geese are known for their silliness not for good judgement.)

233   **lanthorn** lantern

       horned moon new moon, which looks like two horns

234   **He ... head** The mark of a man with an unfaithful wife.

235–6   **He ... circumference** Because he is representing a full moon, there are no horns to be seen.

238   **man i' th' moon** It is supposed to be possible to make out a face in the marks you can see on the moon's surface.

243   **in snuff** about to go out

HIPPOLYTA	It must be your imagination then, and not theirs.
THESEUS	If we imagine no worse of them than they of themselves, they may pass for excellent men. Here come two noble beasts in, a man and a lion.

Enter LION *and* MOONSHINE

LION	You ladies, you, whose gentle hearts do fear	215
	The smallest monstrous mouse that creeps on floor,	
	May now perchance both quake and tremble here.	
	When lion rough in wildest rage doth roar.	
	Then know that I, as Snug the joiner am	
	A lion fell, nor else no lion's dam;	220
	For if I should as lion come in strife	
	Into this place, 'twere pity on my life.	
THESEUS	A very gentle beast, and of a good conscience.	
DEMETRIUS	The very best at a beast, my lord, that e'er I saw.	
LYSANDER	This lion is a very fox for his valour.	225
THESEUS	True; and a goose for his discretion.	
DEMETRIUS	Not so my lord, for his valour cannot carry his discretion, and the fox carries the goose.	
THESEUS	His discretion, I am sure, cannot carry his valour; for the goose carries not the fox. It is well. Leave it to his discretion, and let us listen to the moon.	230
MOONSHINE	This lanthorn doth the horned moon present –	
DEMETRIUS	He should have worn the horns on his head.	
THESEUS	He is no crescent, and his horns are invisible within the circumference.	235
MOONSHINE	This lanthorn doth the horned moon present, Myself the man i' th' moon do seem to be.	
THESEUS	This is the greatest error of all the rest; the man should be put into the lanthorn. How is it else the man i' th' moon?	240
DEMETRIUS	He dares not come there for the candle. For you see, it is already in snuff.	

The story of the play proceeds, still with comments from the audience. Thisby goes to Ninus' tomb to meet Pyramus. Before he arrives a lion frightens her away, but savages her cloak, which Pyramus finds.

247   **must ... time** see the whole play through

261   **Well moused** The lion shakes Thisby's cloak in its jaws as a cat shakes a mouse.

269   **mark** pay attention

HIPPOLYTA   I am aweary of this moon. Would he would change.

THESEUS   It appears by his small light of discretion, that he   245
             is in the wane. But yet, in courtesy, in all reason,
             we must stay the time.

LYSANDER   Proceed Moon.

STARVELING   All that I have to say, is to tell you that the
             lanthorn is the moon, I the man in the moon, this   250
             thorn-bush, my thorn-bush, and this dog my dog.

DEMETRIUS   Why all these should be in the lanthorn; for all
             these are in the moon. But silence, here comes
             Thisby.

             Enter THISBY

THISBY   This is old Ninny's tomb. Where is my love?   255

LION   [*Roars*] Oh –   [THISBY *runs off*

DEMETRIUS   Well roared, Lion.

THESEUS   Well run, Thisby.

HIPPOLYTA   Well shone, Moon. Truly the moon shines
             with a good grace.   [*The* LION *shakes* THISBY'S 260
                                            mantle, and exit

THESEUS   Well moused, Lion.

DEMETRIUS   And then came Pyramus.

LYSANDER   And so the lion vanished.

             Enter PYRAMUS

PYRAMUS   Sweet moon, I thank thee for thy sunny beams.
                 I thank thee, moon, for shining now so bright.   265
             For by thy gracious, golden, glittering gleams,
                 I trust to take of truest Thisby sight.
                     But stay, O spite!
                     But mark, poor knight,
             What dreadful dole is here!   270
                     Eyes do you see?
                     How can it be?
             O dainty duck! O dear!

Pyramus finds blood on the cloak and assumes that something dreadful has happened to Thisby. Overcome with grief, he stabs himself.

276 **Furies** In Greek mythology they were three fierce goddesses who carried out the curses made on murderers and other criminals.

278 **thrum** Each length of the warp thread on a weaving-loom. It is used here for **alliteration** (see Glossary p. 224).

279 **Quail** overcome

quell put to death (The alliteration is more important for the comic effect than the sense.)

280 **passion** grief, outburst

282 **Beshrew** Curse

283 **frame** create

284 **deflowered** violated

285 **dame** lady

286 **cheer** cheerfulness

290 **pap** breast

291 **hop** beat

299 **die** A 'die' is the singular form of 'dice' i.e. one die, two dice. It is used here as a **pun** (see Glossary p. 228) to comment on Pyramus' long-drawn-out death.

ace One spot on a die. Ace too becomes a pun, with reference to 'ass', which is also **dramatic irony** (see Glossary p. 225), since only we know that Bottom was given an ass's head in the wood.

306 **passion** passionate speech

Thy mantle good,
What, stained with blood!   275
Approach ye Furies fell.
O Fates, come, come,
Cut thread and thrum,
Quail, crush, conclude, and quell.

THESEUS This passion, and the death of a dear friend,   280
would go near to make a man look sad.

HIPPOLYTA Beshrew my heart, but I pity the man.

PYRAMUS O wherefore Nature, didst thou lions frame?
Since lion vile hath here deflowered my dear.
Which is – no, no – which was the fairest dame   285
That lived, that loved, that liked, that looked with
    cheer.
Come tears, confound.
Out sword, and wound
The pap of Pyramus;
Ay, that left pap,   290
Where heart doth hop.   [*Stabs himself*
Thus die I, thus, thus, thus
Now am I dead,
Now am I fled,
My soul is in the sky.   295
Tongue lose thy light,
Moon take thy flight,   [*Exit* MOONSHINE
Now die, die, die, die, die.   [*Dies*

DEMETRIUS No die, but an ace for him; for he is but one.

LYSANDER Less than an ace, man; for he is dead, he is nothing.   300

THESEUS With the help of a surgeon he might yet recover,
and prove an ass.

HIPPOLYTA How chance Moonshine is gone before Thisby
comes back and finds her lover?

THESEUS She will find him by starlight. Here she comes,   305
and her passion ends the play.

Enter THISBY

Thisby at first assumes her lover is asleep, but finding he is dead, mourns him in a long speech and then stabs herself to death. Bottom explains the end of the play and then offers an epilogue or a dance.

309   **A mote** The least little thing (literally: speck of dust)

311   **warrant** keep, protect

313   **means** laments, mourns

        videlicet namely (a Latin legal term)

326   **Sisters Three** i.e. the Fates

329   **gore** blood

330   **shore** shorn, cut

334   **imbrue** stain with blood

342   **epilogue** A speech to the audience at the end of a play.

        Bergamask A country dance from Bergamo in Italy.

HIPPOLYTA Methinks she should not use a long one for such
a Pyramus. I hope she will be brief.

DEMETRIUS A mote will turn the balance, which Pyramus,
which Thisby, is the better; he for a man, God   310
warrant us; she for a woman, God bless us.

LYSANDER She hath spied him already with those sweet eyes.

DEMETRIUS And thus she means, videlicet –

THISBY Asleep my love?
What, dead, my dove?   315
O Pyramus, arise.
Speak, speak. Quite dumb?
Dead, dead? A tomb
Must cover thy sweet eyes.
These lily lips,   320
This cherry nose,
These yellow cowslip cheeks,
Are gone, are gone.
Lovers, make moan.
His eyes were green as leeks.   325
O Sisters Three,
Come, come to me,
With hands as pale as milk;
Lay them in gore,
Since you have shore   330
With shears his thread of silk.
Tongue, not a word.
Come, trusty sword;
Come blade, my breast imbrue.   [*Stabs herself*
And farewell, friends,   335
Thus Thisby ends
Adieu, adieu, adieu.   [*Dies*

THESEUS Moonshine and Lion are left to bury the dead.

DEMETRIUS Ay, and Wall too.

BOTTOM [*Starting up*] No, I assure you, the wall is down 340
that parted their fathers. Will it please you to see
the epilogue, or to hear a Bergamask dance

Theseus asks for the dance and praises their play. Bottom and Flute dance the Bergamask and then leave. Theseus says it is past midnight and time for bed. They can look forward to a fortnight of celebrations. When the humans have gone, Puck comes in. Night is the time for spirits and he has been sent, with broom in hand, to get things ready for the fairies.

347   **writ** wrote

350   **discharged** performed

SD   *A **dance*** Bottom and Flute dance the Bergamask then leave

352   **iron tongue** clapper of the bell

354   **out-sleep** oversleep

355   **overwatched** stayed up too late

356   **palpable-gross** plainly stupid
beguiled charmed away

357   **gait** pace

358   **solemnity** celebration of our wedding

359   **revels** entertainments

361   **behowls** howls at

362   **heavy** tired

363   **fordone** exhausted

364   **wasted brands** burnt-out wood (on the fire)

366–7 **Puts ... shroud** makes someone lying tossing and turning in bed think of death

370   **Every ... sprite** each grave opens up to let its ghost out

373   **triple Hecate** Greek goddess associated with night and with hell, with ghosts and magic. She is often shown as three statues in one.

376   **frolic** playful

377   **hallowed** blessed

between two of our company?

THESEUS   No epilogue, I pray you; for your play needs no
excuse. Never excuse; for when the players are   345
all dead, there need none to be blamed. Marry if
he that writ it had played Pyramus, and hanged
himself in Thisby's garter, it would have been a
fine tragedy. And so it is, truly, and very notably
discharged. But come, your Bergamask. Let your   350
epilogue alone.   [A dance, then exeunt both
The iron tongue of midnight hath told twelve.
Lovers to bed, 'tis almost fairy time.
I fear we shall out-sleep the coming morn,
As much as we this night have overwatched.   355
This palpable-gross play hath well beguiled
The heavy gait of night. Sweet friends, to bed.
A fortnight hold we this solemnity,
In nightly revels, and new jollity.

                                                [Exeunt
           Enter PUCK

PUCK   Now the hungry lion roars,   360
              And the wolf behowls the moon;
           Whilst the heavy ploughman snores,
              All with weary task fordone.
           Now the wasted brands do glow,
              Whilst the screech-owl, screeching loud,   365
           Puts the wretch that lies in woe
              In remembrance of a shroud.
           Now it is the time of night,
              That the graves all gaping wide,
           Every one lets forth his sprite,   370
              In the church-way paths to glide.
           And we fairies, that do run
              By the triple Hecate's team,
           From the presence of the sun,
              Following darkness like a dream,   375
           Now are frolic: not a mouse
           Shall disturb this hallowed house.

Oberon and Titania enter with all their attendants. They are ready, as promised, to sing and dance and bless the palace and the newly-weds sleeping in it. They promise true love and happiness, and children born without any disfigurement. They will dance there until daybreak.

380   **glimmering light** faint, wavering light

381   **drowsy** The fire might still have a few glowing embers, and so be 'sleepy'.

383   **briar** thorny stem

384   **ditty** song

385   **trippingly** lightly

386   **rehearse** repeat

      by rote from memory

391   **stray** wander

394   **issue there create** children created there

398   **blots ... hand** deformities, accidents of birth

401   **mark prodigious** monstrous birthmark

402   **nativity** birth

405   **take his gait** make his way

406   **several** separate

410   **make no stay** don't delay

I am sent with broom before,
To sweep the dust behind the door.

Enter OBERON *and* TITANIA *with their train*

OBERON   Through the house give glimmering light,   380
By the dead and drowsy fire,
Every elf and fairy sprite
Hop as light as bird from briar,
And this ditty after me,
Sing, and dance it trippingly.   385

TITANIA   First rehearse your song by rote,
To each word a warbling note.
Hand in hand, with fairy grace,
Will we sing, and bless this place. [*Song and dance*

OBERON   Now, until the break of day,   390
Through this house each fairy stray.
To the best bride-bed will we,
Which by us shall blessed be.
And the issue there create,
Ever shall be fortunate.   395
So shall all the couples three
Ever true in loving be;
And the blots of Nature's hand
Shall not in their issue stand.
Never mole, hare lip, nor scar,   400
Nor mark prodigious, such as are
Despised in nativity,
Shall upon their children be.
With this field-dew consecrate,
Every fairy take his gait,   405
And each several chamber bless,
Through this palace, with sweet peace;
And the owner of it blest,
Ever shall in safety rest.
Trip away; make no stay;   410
Meet me all by break of day.

[*Exeunt* OBERON, TITANIA, *and train*

Puck gives the epilogue. It is an apology for any offence given, and a suggestion that the audience, too, has in fact been dreaming. He asks for the audience's goodwill and wishes them goodnight.

412 **shadows** fairies, spirits

417 **No ... but** offering no more than

418 **reprehend** find fault with us

419 **mend** do better

421 **unearned luck** luck we have not deserved

422 **'scape** escape

serpent's tongue hisses from the audience

426 **Give ... hands** Clap, applaud us

427 **restore amends** make improvements

EPILOGUE

PUCK   If we shadows have offended,
Think but this, and all is mended,
That you have but slumbered here,
While these visions did appear.   415
And this weak and idle theme,
No more yielding but a dream,
Gentles, do not reprehend.
If you pardon, we will mend.
And, as I am an honest Puck,   420
If we have unearned luck
Now to 'scape the serpent's tongue,
We will make amends ere long;
Else the Puck a liar call.
So, good night unto you all.   425
Give me your hands, if we be friends,
And Robin shall restore amends.

[*Exit*

Act 5

Character: Theseus

We previously met Theseus in Act 1 scene 1 and Act 4 scene 1.

Work on your own

1   Without looking back in the book, jot down as many words as you can to describe your impressions of Theseus.

2   Now think about your answers to these questions:

   a   Why is Theseus marrying Hippolyta, and how does she feel about it?

   b   In Act 1 Egeus demands that his daughter Hermia should be forced to marry Demetrius, even though she is in love with Lysander. How does Theseus respond? What do you think of this?

   c   In Act 4 Egeus makes the same demand. How does Theseus respond this time? What are your feelings about that?

Work with a partner

3   Read again lines 1–105.

4   Make a list of at least five words to describe Theseus' character in this section. You can choose from the list below, or think of your own words. **Warning:** the list also contains some words that do not describe Theseus well.

arrogant	bossy	easily bored	fun-loving
generous	humble	humorous	imaginative
impatient	intelligent	kind	kind-hearted
noble	racist	sarcastic	thoughtful

5   For each of the words you have chosen, find some evidence to support your choice. Copy the table at the top of the next page and use it to record your ideas. Write the line numbers where the evidence is to be found

6   Use the 'Explanation' column to link the word you have chosen and the evidence you have found.

	Word	Evidence	Explanation
1			
2			

Language: 'The lunatic, the lover, and the poet'

In a famous speech in Act 5 scene 1 (lines 4–22) Theseus compares 'lunatics', lovers, and poets.

Work with a partner

1 Copy the table below.

2 Use the spaces on the right to explain briefly in your own words what you think each expression tells us about Theseus' argument.

Lines	What he says	What it tells us
4–6	Lovers and madmen ... comprehends.	Lovers and 'madmen' have so much going on in their heads, all whirling around, that they see many things that calm, 'sane' thinkers do not see.
8	... are of imagination all compact.	
9–10	One sees ... madman.	
10–11	The lover ... Egypt.	
12–13	The poet's eye ... heaven ...	
14–17	... as imagination ... name.	

3 Discuss your table. Make notes on an answer to the question below, so that you can present your answer to the rest of the class.

Why does Theseus say that 'the lunatic, the lover, and the poet' are similar, and how are they different?

Missing the point

In Act 5 Shakespeare pokes fun at badly written plays and ham-fisted actors. The first joke comes when Quince cannot make sense of the lines he has been given as Prologue. In Shakespeare's time, actors didn't have a printed script of the whole play. Instead each actor's part was written out with just the cues to show when they had to speak. They only discovered what the whole play was like when they rehearsed it.

Sometimes the part they were given was not very well written and had very little punctuation. So what Quince got might have looked something like this:

> if we offend it is with our good will that you should think we come not to offend but with good will to show our simple skill that is the true beginning of our end consider then we come but in despite we do not come as minding to contest you our true intent is all for your delight we are not here that you should here repent you the actors are at hand and by their show you shall know all that you are like to know

Work in a group of three or four

1   Without looking back in the book, take it in turns to read this speech aloud. Make as much sense of it as you can.

2   When everyone has had a go, agree on a version and write it out with the correct punctuation.

3   Now look back at the speech (page 169, lines 108–17). Discuss how you think the actor should perform it. For example, it could be:

   a   spoken all in a rush as if s/he is in a hurry to get to the end

   b   spoken very hesitantly as s/he tries to work out what it is supposed to mean

   c   some fast, some slow, as the actor gains confidence and then loses it again.

4   Each try the speech in a different way – but remember to pay attention to the punctuation as it is in the book.

Plot summary quiz

The 12 short quotations below sum up the story of the whole play.

1 Work out the correct order for them.

2 Work out who said each one.

A

I see their knavery. This is to make an ass of me, to fright me, if they could.

B

…she is mine, and all my right of her I do estate unto Demetrius.

C

Give me your hands, if we be friends,
And Robin shall restore amends.

D

…in the temple, by and by, with us
These couples shall eternally be knit.

E

What hempen home-spuns have we swaggering here, So near the cradle of the Fairy Queen?

F

Having once this juice,
I'll watch Titania when she is asleep,
And drop the liquor of it in her eyes.

G

The king doth keep his revels here tonight. Take heed the queen come not within his sight.

H

Tongue lose thy light,
Moon take thy flight,
Now, die, die, die, die, die.

I

I wooed thee with my sword…
But I will wed thee in another key,
With pomp, with triumph, and with revelling.

J

We will meet, and there we may rehearse most obscenely and courageously.

K

Content with Hermia? No, I do repent
The tedious minutes I with her have spent.
Not Hermia, but Helena I love.

L

How came these things to pass?
O, how mine eyes do loathe his visage now.

Act 1

While Theseus, Duke of Athens, and Hippolyta are looking forward to their wedding, Egeus arrives demanding that Theseus forces Egeus' daughter, Hermia, to marry his choice, Demetrius, rather than her choice, Lysander. Theseus supports Egeus, and Hermia and Lysander decide to run away together. Helena, Hermia's friend, is sad because Demetrius doesn't love her. To win his love she decides to tell Demetrius about Lysander's and Hermia's plan to run away. Meanwhile, a group of Athens workmen – including a buffoon called Bottom – meet to plan a play to perform at Theseus' wedding celebrations.

Act 2

Fairy king and queen, Oberon and Titania, quarrel because Titania won't give Oberon a human child she has adopted. To get his way, Oberon uses a potion on Titania to make her fall in love with whatever she next sees. Demetrius threatens Helena to stop her following him. Oberon tells Puck to apply the potion to Demetrius, but by mistake he uses it on Lysander, who falls in love with Helena. She assumes she is being made fun of.

Act 3

The workmen rehearse incompetently in the woods. Puck frightens the players away by putting a donkey's head on Bottom. When Titania sees him she falls in love with him. To correct Puck's earlier mistake, Oberon puts the potion on Demetrius, who also falls in love with Helena. The four lovers meet and quarrel bitterly. Puck uses trickery to stop Demetrius and Lysander killing each other. He then applies an antidote to Lysander.

Act 4

When Titania has made a fool of herself over Bottom and lost interest in her adopted boy, Oberon releases the spell. Out hunting, Theseus finds the four lovers asleep. Because they are now in harmony he overrules Egeus and allows Lysander and Hermia to marry. The lovers feel as if they have been – and still are – dreaming. Bottom wakes in confusion. He rejoins his worried fellow-players and tells them to get ready to perform.

Act 5

Theseus and Hippolyta, Demetrius and Helena, and Lysander and Hermia get married in a triple wedding. The workmen's play is chosen as part of the wedding evening entertainment. Although the play sounds ridiculous Theseus urges everyone to take it in the generous spirit in which it is offered. The performance, which is clumsy and comic, ends with a dance. Theseus orders everyone to bed. Oberon instructs the fairies to bless and protect the newly-weds and to grant them peace and fertility. Puck asks for the audience's pardon and applause.

Act/Scene	Action	Theme/Summary
1.1	Egeus demands Hermia marries Demetrius, not Lysander. Theseus agrees. Helena is sad because Demetrius doesn't love her. Hermia and Lysander to run away.	Personal vs parental choice of marriage partner. What is love? 'The course of true love never did run smooth.'
1.2	Workmen plan a play for Theseus.	Bottom the buffoon?
2.1	Fairy king and queen quarrel over a boy. Oberon schemes to put a spell on Titania and Demetrius to make them fall in love with the first thing they see.	Love and hate. Chaos in the fairy and human worlds.
2.2	Love juice put on Titania and – in error – Lysander, who falls for Helena.	Spiteful Oberon. Love as a sort of madness or torment.
3.1	The players' first rehearsal ends in terror when Puck puts a donkey's head on Bottom. Titania falls in love with him, treats him possessively.	The chaotic, haunted, enchanted woods. Absurd, obsessive love.
3.2	Oberon uses the potion to make Demetrius fall for Helena too. The lovers meet, quarrel, and threaten. Puck charms them to sleep and releases Lysander from the spell.	Tragedy threatens. Love as destructive, divisive, absurd, even life-threatening.
4.1	Having got the boy, Oberon releases Titania. Theseus wakes the lovers, overrules Egeus, and allows their marriages. Bottom wakes in confusion.	Harmony restored to fairy and human worlds. Established authorities back in control.
4.2	The reunited players ready to perform.	Bottom valued after all.
5.1	Theseus on love and imagination. The performance of Pyramus and Thisby is clumsy but appreciated. The evening ends and the fairies bless the lovers.	The power of love and imagination. Mutual respect between ruler and his people. Peace and harmony restored.

In this section of the book there are activities and advice to help you explore the play in more detail:

- Character (pages 196–202)
- Drama and performance (pages 203–7)
- Themes and issues (pages 208–15)
- Writing about *A Midsummer Night's Dream* (pages 216–21)
- Writing tasks and questions (pages 222–3)

On pages 224–30 there is a Glossary, which explains some of the technical terms that are used in the book.

Character

The play's characters and their qualities

The play has many characters, and of course some behave differently at different points in the play. It is a comedy. Nowadays that means it should make us laugh, but in Shakespeare's day the main meaning of 'comedy' was a play that ended happily. However, that happiness is not guaranteed; often characters seem to be led by devious, malicious and even murderous motives.

Work on your own

1   Look at some of the qualities that characters show at various points in the play:

devotion	wisdom	foolishness	cunning
spite	protectiveness	domination	mischief
playfulness	incompetence	loyalty	selfishness

Choose one character who best represents each of the above 12 qualities. Briefly explain your choice of character by referring to things they say and do.

Work in a group of three or four

2   Compare your lists. Discuss the differences and change your lists if you want to.

3   List at least three qualities shown by each of the following six characters:

Theseus   Hippolyta   Egeus
Quince   Demetrius   Oberon

(You do not have to choose from the list of qualities in question 1.)
Explain your choices.

4 Discuss which character is:
   • most honest and trustworthy
   • least honest and trustworthy.

5 Prepare a presentation for the rest of the class setting out your
   ideas. Each point that you make should be supported by referring
   to details in the script.

Character X-ray

Sometimes in *A Midsummer Night's Dream* characters are under the
influence of a potion that alters how they think. However, characters
– like people in real life – sometimes guard their true thoughts
and feelings. This does not always mean they are being devious or
dishonest. It might be that they are being sensitive to the feelings
of others, or that they want to hear what someone else is thinking
without influencing their thoughts.

To see into their minds we can do a sort of character X-ray.

How to make a character X-ray

• Choose one important moment in the play.
• Around the edge of a large sheet of paper write the names of the
  characters who are on stage.
• From each character draw an arrow to the character(s) who they
  are talking or listening to.
• On one side of the arrow summarise what is being said; on the
  other side suggest their true thoughts and feelings.

On the next page is an unfinished example from Act 1 scene 1 lines
79–98.

Work on your own

1 Take a large sheet of paper and copy the diagram.

2 Read Act 1 scene 1 lines 79–98 again.

3 Add more points to the diagram.

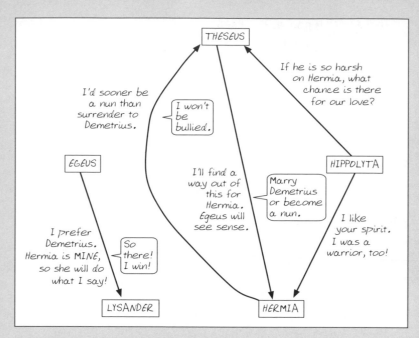

Work with a partner

4 Compare your diagrams and discuss the differences.

5 Choose another point in the play and make a character X-ray for that.

A different approach

You can do a similar exploration using a table. Here is the start of an example for Act 3 scene 2 lines 184–94:

Script	Speaker's thoughts and feelings	Listener(s)' thoughts and feelings
LYSANDER Why should he stay, whom love doth press to go?	How could I ever have loved her? I'll be as harsh as possible to drive her away.	Hermia: What does he mean by that? He must be joking. I don't like the strange look on his face though.
HERMIA What love could		

Work on your own

1 Into the left-hand column copy a short section of dialogue between two or three characters.

2 Use the middle column to jot down the speaker's true thoughts and feelings.

3 Use the right-hand column to jot down the listeners' true thoughts and feelings.

Character interpretation

Actors have to work out what their characters are thinking and feeling in order to interpret them and decide how to play them. They work closely with the director to develop an interpretation. During the performance each member of the audience interprets the characters in their own way. All of this means that in different productions of a play characters can be presented in different ways.

Puck

Puck has been presented in quite different ways. Actors tend to emphasise different interpretations of Puck. For example:

a Puck is a playful mischief-maker.

b Puck is spiteful and scary.

c Puck believes he is very clever but – for a fairy – is actually incompetent and clumsy.

Work on your own

1 Think carefully about the three suggested interpretations of Puck offered above. Draw a table like the one below to explore these three interpretations and what you think of them:

Interpretation	Reasons for	Reasons against	My opinion
a playful			
b spiteful			
c incompetent			

In your opinion, which interpretation is best? Explain your choice. Refer to evidence to support your view.

Work with a partner

2   Compare the tables you have filled in and the interpretation you have chosen as the best one. Discuss differences between your views.

3   Work together on Act 3 scene 2 lines 88–121. One of you takes the part of Puck, the other Oberon.

4   Perform this section three times with Puck's performance being guided by each of the three interpretations in turn: playful, spiteful, incompetent.

5   When you have finished, discuss which interpretation is best, and why.

Work on your own

6   Read Puck's epilogue that ends the play (Act 5 scene 1 lines 411–27).

7   Think about the exploratory work you have already done on Puck. Now write 100–200 words on this two-part question:

   a   What impressions of Puck are we left with at the end of the play?

   b   To what extent do these impressions differ from impressions we get of Puck earlier in the play?

The workmen players

The best way to explore characters is to try them out in different ways. For example, here are two different sets of performance guidelines for the workmen players in Act 3 scene 1 lines 6–67:

	Bottom	The other players
Version 1	You are very enthusiastic and love the sound of your own voice. You think you should have been directing, not Quince. You often stammer.	You know Bottom well and tried to keep this play secret from him. You are fed up with him always taking over. You humour him or you would never be able to get anywhere.

Version 2	You are arrogant and insensitive to others. You are self-seeking and want recognition.	You dislike Bottom, but know he gets things done. You do your best to tolerate him.

Work in a group of six

1 Cast the parts.

2 Read your performance guidelines for Version 1.

3 Read the text of Act 3 scene 1 lines 6–67 and think about how you will perform it, following your guidelines.

4 Rehearse the scene.

5 Now do the same for Version 2.

6 Discuss the two versions: which did you think was more effective and why?

Extension

Choose another short section of the play to try out in different ways. For example: Act 5 scene 1 lines 32–105. Before you start rehearsing, agree two sets of contrasting performance guidelines.

Texting the lovers

The four lovers are the characters we probably get to know best during the play. It is worth considering how the audience might feel about them at different points in the play. For example, we might feel one way about Helena in Act 1 when she tells us about her feelings of rejection, but we might feel quite differently about her in Act 2 scene 1 lines 188–244 when she seems willing to accept Demetrius' abuse in return for the chance to be near him.

Imagine if you could send Helena a text message at that point in the play. What would you say?

The advantage of a text message is that it forces you to be precise and succinct in your response to a character at one point in the play.

Work on your own

1   Imagine that you can send a text message to Demetrius at different stages in the play. You want to tell him what you think of him and/or give him some advice.

2   Send him a text message at each of the following three moments:

   a   Act 2 scene 1 lines 188–237 (threatening Helena)

   b   Act 3 scene 2 lines 322–38 (challenging Lysander)

   c   Act 5 scene 1 lines 224–54 (mocking the workmen–players)

3   Now do the same for one of the other lovers:

   Lysander

   a   Act 2 scene 2 lines 35–65 (settling down in the wood with Hermia)

   b   Act 3 scene 2 lines 249–81 (hating Hermia)

   c   Act 4 scene 1 lines 139–59 (explaining to Theseus)

   Hermia

   a   Act 1 scene 1 lines 46–90 (refusing to marry Demetrius)

   b   Act 3 scene 2 lines 41–81 (accusing Demetrius)

   c   Act 3 scene 2 lines 282–328 (turning against Helena)

   Helena

   Choose three moments of your own.

4   Choose one of the four lovers. Consider the information and understanding you have built up by doing the text message exercise above.

   Explain how the audience's view of that character might vary and develop during the play.

   a   Write at least 200 words.

   b   Focus your answer on three or four parts of the play.

   c   Refer closely to evidence in the play to back up your ideas.

Drama and performance

Hot-seating

Hot-seating is a good way to get inside a character. It is an effective way to prepare for acting. This is how it works:

1 Arrange the chairs in a semi-circle, with one chair at its centre. This is the 'hot seat'.

2 One student plays the part of a character in a particular scene. S/he sits in the hot seat.

3 Students take it in turns to ask the character in the hot seat questions about how they are feeling, why they said or did certain things, and so on.

4 The student in the hot seat has to answer these questions in role and without too much delay. (Their answers can be imaginative but they must make sense in terms of what we know from the play.)

Example: Act 3 scene 2 lines 122–343

Here are some questions Helena might be asked in the hot seat:

• What made you think that the other three were in league with each other to wind you up?

• How did Demetrius' behaviour make you feel about him?

• Why did you keep referring to Hermia's height when you must have known that it would upset her?

Scenes for hot-seating

Act 5 scene 1

Theseus is in the hot seat. You could explore his attitude: is he ever mocking the actors?

Act 4 scene 1 lines 103–86

Hippolyta is in the hot seat. How does she feel about things that are said in this section?

Tableau (or 'freeze-frame')

A tableau is like a film with the pause button pressed, so the actors freeze into position at a particular moment. Here's how to do it:

1 You work in a group of four to six.

2 Cast the parts, with one member of your group as the director. Their job is to help the actors to achieve the agreed expressions and postures.

3 Act out a scene and 'freeze' at different moments. The director could photograph these moments to discuss later.

4 Prepare freeze-frames for other groups to see and comment on.

5 The audience can be asked to:

a work out which moment in the play has been frozen

b what the tableau tells them about this moment in the play.

Abstract tableaux

A tableau can be used in a more abstract way, to express a mood or idea. For example:

- to express Helena's feelings at the end of Act 1 scene 1
- to explore Theseus' idea of 'noble respect' towards the players (Act 5 scene 1 line 91).

The play is full of vivid images. For example:

- **Act 1 scene 1 lines 69–73**
  The image of Hermia as a 'barren' nun
- **Act 2 scene 1 lines 127–34**
  A pregnant woman as a trading ship under full sail

Work in a group of four to six

1 Choose one of the ideas above.

2 Create a freeze-frame for your chosen image.

3 Find two other examples of vivid images.

4 Create freeze-frames for those images.

Statues and sculptures

Rulers such as Theseus often commission statues to mark great events or to celebrate important individuals. Getting together to create a living statue is another good opportunity to discuss a particular aspect of the play.

Who commissions the statue will surely have an influence on the statue. For example, Theseus and Egeus would presumably want to commemorate the marriage of Hermia and Lysander in different ways.

Work in a small group

1 Choose a statue from the list below.

2 Read the section of the play referred to.

3 Decide what feelings and ideas you want this statue to convey.

4 Cast the parts. The rest of the group are the sculptors.

5 The sculptors now create the statue.

Subject	Commissioned by	Point in the play
Hippolyta	Theseus	the lead-up to their wedding at the end of Act 5 scene 1
Theseus	the workmen–players	the end of the play
Theseus	Hippolyta	the end of the play
Hermia and Lysander	Egeus	the end of the play
The players	Theseus	the end of the play

6 Now choose a different moment in the play (i.e. not one of those in the table).

7 Decide who is commissioning the statue and what it shows.

8 Sculpt your statue.

9 Look at other groups' statues. Decide who they are statues of, and at what point in the play.

Stepping out of the text

This is another way of exploring characters and bringing them to life. You ask yourself what those characters would be like in other situations – even impossible ones.

The golden rule is what the characters say and do must be justified by what we know of them from Shakespeare's script. In other words, they must stay in role.

Examples

1 Imagine that Theseus makes a Christmas speech on Athens TV. Write and/or deliver Theseus' speech.

2 Imagine that Egeus comes to stay with his daughter, Hermia, and her husband a year later.
   Act out or write a dialogue between the three of them.

Decision alley

Decision alley is a way of exploring some of the options that are open to characters (and the playwright) at certain points in the play. It works best for moments in the play when a character is wrestling with their conscience to make a decision.

Here is how a decision alley works:

1 You choose a particular moment in the play and decide who is the key character at that moment.

2 One person plays the key character.

3 The rest of the class stands in two lines facing each other down the length of the room.

4 Each person in the alley thinks of some brief advice they would like to give the character about what s/he should do at this point in the play.

5 The character walks slowly down the alley, pausing by each person in the alley to hear their advice.

6 When the person playing the character reaches the end of the alley they should think aloud about the advice they have been given and explain what they have decided to do now.

'But soft, what nymphs are these?'

Towards the end of Act 4 scene 1 (lines 139–86), Theseus has to decide what to do when he finds the lovers together. You could use a decision alley to help him decide. Each person in the alley could be one of the other characters present.

Think about the advice each might give and then do a decision alley.

Production design

When *A Midsummer Night's Dream* was first produced, plays were generally performed in daylight. The section about Shakespeare's Theatre on pages 19–22 describes what a theatre probably looked like, with several drawings. The Globe Theatre was round and only partly covered by a roof. Look carefully at the stage and where it is in relation to the audience.

Discussion points

1   What challenges might Shakespeare's acting company have faced when it came to performing *A Midsummer Night's Dream*?

2   What advantages did they have?

3   What advantages do modern professional theatres have when producing the play?

4   Do modern theatres have any disadvantages?

A school production

Work in a group of three to five

1   Imagine that the play is being performed by students in your own school.

2   Decide where the play will be performed.

3   Do a sketch of the acting and audience area. You should be both practical and imaginative in this.

4   Choose one scene from the play and write detailed advice on how it should be performed. A good way to do this would be to get a copy of the scene and write your advice alongside the script.

You could mention any or all of the following:

acting	speaking	lighting
music	sound	costumes
props	scenery	movement

Themes and issues

Love as romance

Shakespeare has included a number of traditional elements that help create an intensely romantic atmosphere. Here are some of those elements:

- the passionate feelings of the young lovers
- the fact that the core of the action takes place in moonlight in the summer
- the rhyming poetry used by the young lovers in many of their speeches
- conflict between young people and their parents over who is a suitable choice of partner.

Work on your own

1 Copy out the list above.

2 Add at least two more things that give the play a romantic atmosphere.

3 Look at your list of romantic love elements. For each one write down one or two examples from the play. Here is an example:

> The passionate feelings of the young lovers
>
> a Lysander and Hermia run away together because they are so in love with each other.
>
> b Helena is helplessly in love with Demetrius; she wants nothing but to be with him. '...I am sick when I look not on you.' (Act 2 scene 1 line 213)

4 Although it is often ridiculous, the workmen's play *Pyramus and Thisby*, echoes the romantic elements. For example, it dramatises the conflict between young lovers and their parents.

Look again at your list of romantic elements. Choose three of them and explain how *Pyramus and Thisby* uses those three elements. Write a paragraph for each of your three elements.

Hermia and Lysander

Hermia's father, Egeus, might well appear to be selfish and unreasonable, but do Hermia and Lysander behave wisely?

Work on your own

Imagine that at the end of Act 1 scene 1 Hermia writes to a magazine problem page for advice. She tells the 'agony aunt' about her feelings for Lysander, her father's attitude and what she plans to do.

Write the agony aunt's reply that is published in the magazine. Before you begin, think about:

- Hermia's problem
- what might be the consequences of running away
- other ways she could deal with her problem
- what sort of advice would be wise in these circumstances.

Love as madness

Love can make people behave in completely irrational ways, and at least three of the characters realise this:

- Puck, the 'mad spirit' (Act 3 scene 2 line 4), is the agent of much of the chaos and madness in the wood. Puck enjoys tormenting people and is fully aware of the connection between love and madness. He is delighted that 'Cupid is a knavish lad, | Thus to make poor females mad' (Act 3 scene 2 lines 440–1).
- Meanwhile, Bottom points out (with accidental wisdom), 'reason and love keep little company together now-a-days' (Act 3 scene 1 lines 137–8).
- Theseus observes the similarity between 'lovers and madmen': they both 'have such seething brains' (Act 5 scene 1 line 4).

The love juice controls who people love, but it doesn't account for how they behave.

Work on your own

1 Reread Act 3 scene 2.

2 Make notes about how the behaviour of the four lovers could be considered irrational, or even mad.

3 Find some details in the script to support your ideas.

Work in a group of three

4 Take it in turns to present to each other your work on questions 2 and 3.

5 Read Theseus' comparison of lovers and madmen in Act 5 scene 1 lines 7–17 (from 'The lunatic...' down to '...and a name').

Work on your own

6 In your own words, summarise the similarities that Theseus notices between poets, lovers, and madmen.

Love as sickness

We sometimes say that someone is 'love sick' and in that phrase we recognise similarities between being in love and being ill. Oberon says of Helena:

> *All fancy-sick she is and pale of cheer,*
> *With sighs of love, that costs the fresh blood dear...*
> (Act 3 scene 2 lines 96–7)

The love-as-sickness idea is developed elsewhere in the play. For example, when Oberon puts love juice on Demetrius' eyes he tells him:

> *When thou wakest, if she be by,*
> *Beg of her for remedy.*
> (Act 3 scene 2 lines 108–9)

When Demetrius suddenly falls in love with Helena he explains that '... like a sickness, did I loathe this food' (Act 4 scene 1 line 173).

Work on your own

1 Find the three quotations listed above.

2 Carefully read each quotation and the lines surrounding it.

3 For each quotation write a short explanation of how Shakespeare makes a connection between love and illness. Refer closely to Shakespeare's choice of language.

4 Find at least one more quotation that connects love and illness, and explain how Shakespeare's words make that connection. You can choose your own quotations but you will find a useful one in Act 2 scene 1.

Love as folly

People have always made fools of themselves over love and this is precisely what Puck finds so entertaining. He asks Oberon:

> *Shall we their fond [foolish] pageant see?*
> *Lord, what fools these mortals [humans] be!*
> (Act 3 scene 2 lines 114–15)

Helena

Love appears to be a folly when it is obsessive or one-sided. Shakespeare often uses the word 'dote' to signal this sort of love. Lysander insists to Egeus that Helena:

> *...sweet lady, dotes,*
> *Devoutly dotes, dotes in idolatry,*
> *Upon this spotted and inconstant man.*
> (Act 1 scene 1 lines 108–10)

The words 'devoutly' and 'idolatry' emphasise Helena's folly: she worships Demetrius like a false god.

Work with a partner

At the end of Act 2 scene 1 Demetrius tells Helena that he cannot stand her and then leaves her alone in the wood. What advice might a good friend give her? Would it be to forget Demetrius because he isn't worth it? What would Helena reply?

1 One of you should take the part of Helena; the other should be Helena's friend (not Hermia).

2 Work together on the dialogue between Helena and her friend. Helena should explain:
   - her problem
   - her feelings
   - what she intends to do.

3 Perform your dialogue for another pair or for the class. What impression of Helena does your dialogue give?

211

Work on your own

4   Watch others perform their dialogues. As you watch, make notes
    on these questions:

    a   What impressions of Helena are given by their versions of the
    dialogue between Helena and her friend?

    b   How are the impressions of Helena different from those given
    by your own version?

5   Write answers to the questions below. Refer to details in the text
    to support your ideas.

    a   How might the audience feel about Helena during the early
    part of the play up until Act 2 scene 1 line 244?

    b   Other than Helena's love for Demetrius, what examples of
    foolish, obsessive love can you find in the play?

6   Find in the script the three quotations below. Carefully read them
    and the speeches they come from. For each quotation explain:

- who says it and why
- how it is likely to make the audience feel about the speaker
  and characters who are being spoken about.

    a   *The juice of it on sleeping eyelids laid,*
    Will make or man or woman madly dote
    Upon the next live creature that it sees.
    (Act 2 scene 1 lines 170–2)

    b   *To Athens will I bear my folly back,*
    And follow you no further. Let me go.
    You see how simple and how fond I am.
    (Act 3 scene 2 lines 315–17)

    c   *O, how I love thee! How I dote on thee!*
    (Act 4 scene 1 line 45)

Illusion and reality

Characters in the play often think they see one thing when they are
actually seeing something quite different. A clear example of this is
Titania's delusion over Bottom. She calls him an 'angel' (Act 3 scene 1
line 123) and 'beautiful' (line 142), but in reality he is – in Puck's words

– 'a monster' (Act 3 scene 2 line 6). Titania's 'sight' has been altered by the love juice.

Work on your own

1 Find at least four examples in the play of reality and illusion becoming confused.

2 For each example explain:

   a what the confusion is and why it occurs

   b how that confusion affects what happens in the play.

   You could include these examples:

   • The 'trickery' described by Egeus in Act 1
   • The effects of the love juice
   • The players' plans for presenting the moon
   • Tricks that Puck plays.

Theseus

People's failure to tell illusion from reality fascinates Theseus. He notes that people see what they want or fear to see. He talks about the 'tricks' that imagination plays (Act 5 scene 1 line 18).

Work on your own

1 Read Act 5 scene 1 lines 18–22 to see what Theseus thinks about the power of the imagination.

2 Explain the point that Theseus is making in these lines.

3 Do you think Theseus is right about the effects of the imagination?

Work with a partner

4 Share your answers to 2 and 3 above. Add to or change what you have already written if you need to.

Illusion

Illusion is central to the play's title. Dreams are a common form of illusion. When the lovers' attachments are finally sorted out at the end of Act 4 scene 1, they are left feeling uncertain about what is real and what is merely imagined. 'It seems to me,' says Demetrius, 'That yet we sleep, we dream' (lines 193–4). Many productions of the play seek to work a dream-like quality into every scene.

Work on your own

Imagine you are directing a version of *A Midsummer Night's Dream* to be performed by your fellow-students. Choose one scene from the play and explain in detail your ideas for creating a dream-like quality.

You could refer to any or all of the following:

- use of trickery
- advice to actors
- movement on the stage
- use of music and sound
- use of lighting
- scenery and props.

Enchantment and magic

Work with a partner

1 You are going to work on two speeches:

   a Oberon's speech that begins, 'What thou seest when thou dost wake...' (Act 2 scene 2 lines 27–34)

   b Puck's speech that begins, 'Through the forest have I gone...' (Act 2 scene 2 lines 66–83).

   One of you should be Oberon, the other Puck. Take it in turns to read your speech aloud. Help each other to read so that the rhythms of the speeches are clear.

2 Discuss how the way these speeches are written helps to create a mood of enchantment. You might like to consider how the following things interact and help the mood:

   - rhyme
   - rhythm
   - line length.

The course of true love

Even before they escape to the woods the lovers use a sort of enchanted language when talking to each other about their ill-fortunes. There is, for example, an entranced, call-and-response quality to this conversation between Lysander and Hermia:

LYSANDER	The course of true love never did run smooth;
	But, either it was different in blood –
HERMIA	O cross! Too high to be enthralled to low.
LYSANDER	Or else misgraffed in respect of years –
HERMIA	O spite! Too old to be engaged to young.
LYSANDER	Or else it stood upon the choice of friends –
HERMIA	O hell! To choose love by another's eyes.

(Act 1 scene 1 lines 134–40)

Work in a group of three

1 Work on the lines above. Two of you should play the parts of Lysander and Hermia. The third member of your group should help the actors to speak and act the lines in a way that emphasises their entranced quality.

You should plan – amongst other things – for:

- tone of voice
- pace and rhythm
- actions.

Join up with another group

2 Show each other your performances of these lines and discuss differences in your methods of performance.

Work on your own

3 Choose one short section of the play (up to one page in length) in which magic and enchantment are strong.

a Explain what gives that section its magic and enchantment.

b If you were directing the play how would you try to make the magic and enchantment effective for an audience?

4 Choose another section of the play. Write about how Shakespeare's choice of words and/or his poetry help create a magical, enchanted mood. You could refer to all or some of these elements:

- Shakespeare's choice of words
- images used
- rhythm and/or rhyme
- repetition of words or sounds.

Writing about *A Midsummer Night's Dream*

When you write about the play – even in a test – you should work through six stages:

1 Read the question and make sense of it.
2 Develop your ideas.
3 Plan.
4 Write.
5 Edit your writing.
6 Check that your writing is accurate.

Step 1: Read

The purpose of an assessment task is to let you explore an aspect of the play in detail. In doing that you should show:

• your understanding of the play
• your appreciation of how it has been written and put together
• some idea of the play's relevance to its own time or ours.

You cannot write well about the play unless you understand the task fully. Look at this task:

> To what extent does the play support Bottom's belief that 'reason and love keep little company together now-a-days'?
> (Act 3 scene 1 lines 137–8)

The first thing to do is to identify the key words in the question. These are the words which show you exactly what the question is about.

> To what extent does the play support Bottom's belief that 'reason and love keep little company together now-a-days'?
> (Act 3 scene 1 lines 137–8)

Now the point of the question becomes clear: it is about how much feelings of love cloud a lover's judgement in the play.

Step 2: Develop

Even in a test it is better to spend a few minutes planning your writing rather than rushing straight into it. Before you can make a plan, you need to develop your ideas. Start by writing down the question's key words on a clean page.

Then jot down thoughts that might be relevant to those key words. Here is part of an example:

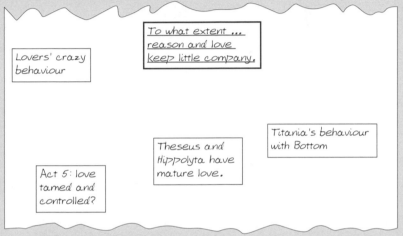

Now use lines to mark possible links between your thoughts like this:

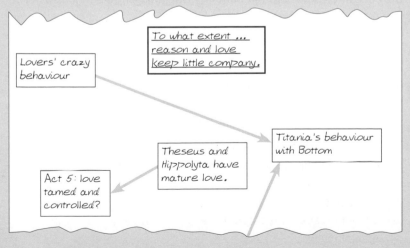

Add pieces of evidence (for example, short quotations) that you might be able to use in your writing to support your ideas:

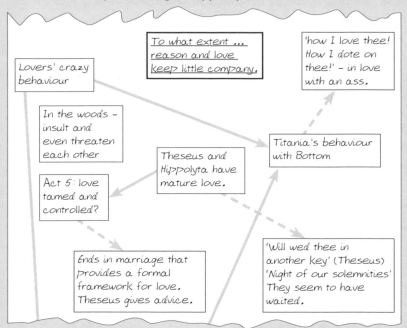

Keeping adding detail, references, ideas and links between them as they occur to you. Thorough planning will make writing much easier and more successful.

Step 3: Plan

Now you need to shape your ideas into a plan. This will ensure that your writing has a good structure, or order, and that it remains relevant to the task.

1   You need an introduction that explains:

   a   what the task means for you

   b   why this topic is an important one.

Think about the various ways in which the play shows love to be impulsive and irrational. However, don't answer the question yet; just get your reader interested! Here is an example of a lively and engaging opening:

> Bottom is given an ass' head by Puck, but the joke is that he was always an ass – a fool. However, when he observes that love and reason seldom go together, the play's audience are likely to agree. They have seen good friends fall out and threaten to assault or even kill each other in the name of love. They have also seen lovers make fools of themselves as they fall in and out of passionate love at a moment's notice. By accident, Bottom might be the wisest character in the play!

2 At the end of the answer you need a concluding paragraph. This sums up your most important points and answers the question directly. Here you might consider whether love seems more reasonable at the end of the play than earlier on.

3 Now for the tricky part: you need a sequence of paragraphs that bridge the gap between the introduction and the conclusion. Look back at the question and at the ideas you have come up with. From these you should be able to pick out some useful paragraph topics and a sensible order for those paragraphs.

Here is a possible paragraph sequence for your essay:

Paragraph	Topic of paragraph	Focus
1	Introduction	Grab your reader's interest relevantly.
2	The power struggle in the first scene. Lack of compromise.	Act 1 scene 1
3	The effects of the love-juice on what the lovers say and do.	Love vs hate, especially Act 3 scene 2
4	Titania and Bottom	Folly/doting (compare with Helena)
5	The love between Theseus and Hippolyta: 'musical discord'.	Act 1 scene 1; Act 4 scene 1 (lines 103– 86)
6	Impression of love given by Act 5: role of marriage.	Love tamed and blessed. Mutual respect stressed.
7	Conclusion	Answer the question.

Step 4: Draft

Whatever the writing task, you need to explore as many of these things as you can:

- The play's ideas and meaning
- Its structure
- Its characters
- Audience (or reader) reaction
- Stagecraft: how the play could be performed
- The language of the play.

Point, Evidence, and Explanation

It is easy to become vague when you are writing. Planning will help you to stick to the point and to organise your ideas so that you develop and explain them rather than keep repeating them.

PEE – point, evidence, explanation – is a useful formula for expressing your ideas clearly. Here is an example related to paragraph 4 of the essay outline on page 219:

> Like Helena's love for Demetrius, Titania's love for Bottom is a foolish obsession [POINT]. 'How I dote on thee!' Titania exclaims to the sleeping Bottom. (Act 4 scene 1 line 45) [EVIDENCE] The word 'dote' suggests that Titania is infatuated with Bottom and it reminds us of Lysander's account of Helena's feelings for Demetrius: she 'dotes,/Devoutly dotes, dotes in idolatry' on him (Act 1 scene 1 lines 108-9). Perhaps Shakespeare is signalling through the word 'dote' that their love is dangerous to themselves. [EXPLANATION]

To explore ideas and evidence try to use words such as 'could', 'might', 'perhaps'. These help you explore more than one possibility – as in the example above.

Step 5: Edit

When you have finished your first draft you should read through it carefully to make sure it actually says what you mean. As you read it through, try to imagine that you are the person who will mark it. What would they think of what you have written? Ask yourself:

- Have I explored ideas and considered alternatives?
- Are my sentences clear and to the point, or are they vague?
- Have I missed out anything crucial?
- Is everything relevant to the task?
- Make any changes needed.

Step 6: Check

When you are satisfied with your answer, make a final check for:

- grammar
- punctuation
- spelling.

Writing tasks and questions

Each of the following varied writing tasks should allow you to show:

- your understanding of the play
- your appreciation of how it has been written and put together (language and structure)
- some idea of the play's relevance to its own time or ours.

1 Choose two sections of the play which are full of conflict. Between them, your chosen sections should feature both conflict in the fairy world and in the human world.

Carefully explore how the battle between conflict and harmony is presented in those two sections of the play.

2 • Act 1 scene 2
- Act 3 scene 1 lines 1–101
- Act 4 scene 2

What advice would you give to the actors in these three sections of the play to help them show the relationship between Bottom and the rest of the players?

3 Imagine that at Act 2 scene 2 line 65, with the help of the fairies' magic, Hermia time-travels into the early twenty-first century. After she has lived in our time for a while she writes a letter home. Write Hermia's letter home from the twenty-first century.

4 At the end of Act 4 scene 1, Bottom thinks he has been dreaming. He decides to 'get Peter Quince to write a ballad of...Bottom's Dream'. In ballad or story form write Peter Quince's Bottom's Dream.

5 Act 2 scene 1 lines 188–244

  a From this extract, what do you learn about Helena?

  b To what extent is Helena similar or different in the rest of the play?

6 Choose **one** key theme in *A Midsummer Night's Dream*. Compare your reading of the theme with how that theme is presented in a performance of the play that you have seen.

7 In *A Midsummer Night's Dream*, how does Shakespeare exploit for comic effect the absurdities of people in love?

8 How does the workmen's play, *Pyramus and Thisby*, parallel events and themes in the main play?

9 Hippolyta rarely speaks in those scenes where she is on stage. What does she think about what people say and do?

Write Hippolyta's diary entry at the following three points in the play:

- Act 1 scene 1 line 127
- Act 4 scene 1 line 186
- The end of the play

10 How might an audience's reactions to Puck and Oberon vary at different points in the play?

In your answer concentrate in detail on at least three different sections of the play.

11 Presumably at the end of the play Egeus has given his blessing to the marriage of Hermia and Lysander. Did he give this willingly?

Imagine that Athens TV news runs an extended interview with Egeus after the triple wedding. They ask him about his attitude towards the wedding and the events that led up to it.

Write the script of the interview.

Glossary

In these explanations, words that are in **bold** type are explained separately in the Glossary.

alliteration   a figure of speech in which a number of words close to each other in a piece of writing begin with the same consonant sound: 'Whereat, with blade, with bloody blameful blade,/ He bravely broached his boiling bloody breast' (Act 5 scene 1 lines 145–6). Quince's repetition of 'b' sounds is an example of clumsy alliteration.

apostrophe   a figure of speech in which a character speaks directly to a person who is not present or to a **personification**. For example, after Titania walks out on her argument with Oberon in Act 2 scene 1, Oberon says to her, 'Well, go thy way' (line 146).

aside   a speech made by one of the characters for the ears of the audience alone, or purely for the benefit of another character on stage. For example, when Puck happens upon the workmen's secret rehearsals in the wood, he asks the audience, 'What hempen home-spuns have we swaggering here?' (Act 3 scene 1 line 73). See also **soliloquy**.

blank verse   Shakespeare wrote his plays using a mixture of prose and verse. The lines of verse sometimes **rhymed** but more often did not rhyme. Verse that does not rhyme is called blank verse.

caesura   a pause or interruption in the middle of a line of verse (from the Latin word meaning 'to cut'). In Act 3 scene 2 Demetrius challenges Lysander:
Thou runaway, thou coward, art thou fled?
Speak! In some bush? Where dost thou hide thy head?
(lines 405–6)
The broken, jerky lines reflect Demetrius' mood.

contraction   shortening a word or words by missing out some of the letters. The missing letters are shown by an apostrophe. Modern examples are she's (for she is) and shan't (for shall not). In Shakespeare's time other contractions were also used, such as 'tis (for it is) and show'st (for showest).

dramatic irony   a situation in a play when the audience (and possibly some of the characters) know something one or more of the characters do not. In a pantomime, for example, young children will often shout to tell the hero that a dreadful monster is creeping up behind him, unseen. In Act 3 scene 1 Bottom accuses his friends of trying to 'make an ass of' him, not realising that he really has been made into an ass.

end-on staging   a form of staging in which the audience sit in rows all facing the same way with the stage at one end.

enjambement   sometimes in blank verse there is a natural pause at the end of a line. At other times there is no break and the sentence just runs over onto the next line. This running on is called enjambement (from the French word for 'span').

exeunt   a Latin word meaning 'They go away', used for the departure of characters from a scene.

exit   a Latin word meaning 'He (or she) goes away', used for the departure of a character from a scene.

extended image   most **images** are fairly short, taking up no more than a line or two. Sometimes a writer builds up an image so that it runs on for several lines. This is called an extended image. At the end of Act 1 scene 1 Helena develops a comparison between Demetrius' feelings and weather processes:
He hailed down oaths that he was only mine;
And when this hail some heat from Hermia felt,
So he dissolved, and showers of oaths did melt.
(lines 243–5)

figurative language   language that is being used so that what is written or said is not literally true, usually for some kind of special effect. **Metaphors** and **similes** are examples of figurative language. When Helena refers to herself and Hermia as 'Two lovely berries moulded on one stem' (Act 3 scene 2 line 211) she means it figuratively rather than literally.

hyperbole   Deliberate exaggeration, for dramatic effect. For example, Lysander insults Hermia by exaggerating her lack of height and calling her 'you dwarf' (Act 3 scene 2 line 328).

iambic pentameter   a line of **verse** which contains ten syllables, with a repeated pattern of weak and strong beats:
For aye to be in shady cloister mewed,
To live a barren sister all your life...
(Act 1 scene 1 lines 71–2)
See also **metre, rhythm**.

imagery   **figurative language** in which the writer communicates an idea by creating a picture in the mind of the reader or listener. Types of figurative language include **metaphors** and **similes**.

irony   When someone says one thing and means another. Sometimes it is used to tease or satirise someone, or it can express great bitterness. For example, in Act 5 scene 1, Theseus sees Snug and Starveling come on in the workmen's play and says, 'Here come two noble beasts in, a moon and a lion.' He doesn't expect to be taken seriously; he is speaking ironically – they are far from being 'noble'. See also **dramatic irony**.

malapropism a wrong word that sounds like the right one. The players often do this, making nonsense of their speeches. For example, Bottom uses 'odious' when he means 'odours' (Act 3 scene 1 line 78) and presumably he doesn't really mean that they will rehearse 'most obscenely'! (Act 1 scene 2 lines 101–2)

metaphor a figure of speech in which one person, or thing, or idea is described as if it were another. For example, in Act 1 scene 1 Helena sighs that Hermia's 'eyes are lode-stars' to Demetrius (line 183). This metaphor dramatically suggests Hermia's eyes are as bright and enticing as stars that guide us through the night.

metre the regular pattern of weak and strong beats in a line of verse. The commonest metre in Shakespeare's plays is iambic. Each section consists of two syllables. The first is weak and the second is strong. See **iambic pentameter**.

myth a traditional story, often very old. Myths often explain important events in the life of a people and they usually refer to the lives of gods or other supernatural creatures.

onomatopoeia using words that are chosen because they mimic the sound of what is being described.

oxymoron figurative language in which the writer combines two ideas which are opposites. This frequently has a startling or unusual effect. For example, in Act 5 scene 1 Theseus laughs over the oxymorons in the players' description of their play: 'Merry and tragical? Tedious and brief?' (line 58)

personification referring to a thing or an idea as if it were a person. When Oberon blesses the newly-weds at the end of the play he refers to 'Nature's hand' (Act 5 scene 1 line 398). By giving Nature a hand Oberon is personifying it.

play on words see **pun**.

prose the form of language that is used for normal written communication. It is contrasted with **verse**.

proverb a common saying that is used by many people. Proverbs usually express something that is useful knowledge, or that people think is useful. For example, 'Many hands make light work'. Shakespeare often uses proverbs in his plays.

pun a figure of speech in which the writer uses a word that has more than one meaning. Both meanings of the word are used to make a joke or humorous comment. For example, in Act 2 scene 1, when Demetrius says, 'And here am I, and wood within this wood' he is using the word 'wood' in two different ways. It means a large area covered in trees, but in Shakespeare's day it also meant 'mad'.

rhetorical question a question used for effect, usually in an argument or debate, sometimes in a **soliloquy**. An answer is not expected. It would break the flow of the speech if it were offered. For example, Hermia conveys her distress through a series of rhetorical questions:
What, can you do me greater harm than hate?
Hate me, wherefore? O me, what news, my love?
Am not I Hermia? Are not you Lysander?
(Act 3 scene 2 lines 271–3)

rhyme
when two lines of **verse** end with the same sound, they are said to rhyme. Over half of *A Midsummer Night's Dream* is written in rhyming lines. For more about this, see pages 24–5.

rhythm
the pattern of weak and strong syllables in a piece of writing. Shakespeare writes in **iambic pentameters**, but varies the way he uses them by breaking the rules. So his lines are mainly regular but with a lot of small variations. This combination makes up the rhythm of the verse.

satire
making fun of something that you dislike or wish to criticise, by sending it up in some way. For example, Philostrate's description of *Pyramus and Thisby* (Act 5 scene 1 lines 61–70).

simile
a comparison between two things which the writer makes clear by using words such as 'like' or 'as'. In Act 4 scene 1 Demetrius uses a sequence of similes to explain his renewed love for Helena. His love for Hermia is 'Melted as the snow' (line 166).

soliloquy
when a character is alone on stage, or separated from the other characters in some way and speaks either apparently to himself or herself, or directly to the audience. Helena delivers a soliloquy to the audience at the end of Act 1 scene 1. This soliloquy fulfils some typical functions: it creates a feeling of intimacy between a main character and the audience; it provides information about Helena's past and her thoughts; it comments on the play's love theme; and it gives the cast time to get the next scene ready.

theatre-in-the-round
a form of theatre in which the audience sit all round the acting area.

thrust stage   a form of theatre in which the stage projects out into the audience, who thus sit on three sides of it. Shakespeare's Globe Theatre was like this, and so are the modern one in London, and the new Royal Shakespeare Theatre in Stratford-upon-Avon.

verse   writing that uses regular patterns, such as **metre** and **rhyme**.